UNBORED GAMES

SERIOUS FUN
FOR EVERYONE

JOSHUA GLENN & ELIZABETH FOY LARSEN

DESIGN BY TONY LEONE

ILLUSTRATIONS BY MISTER REUSCH &
HEATHER KASUNICK

CHAPTER LETTERING BY CHRIS PIASCIK

B L O O M S B U R Y
NEW YORK · LONDON · NEW DELHI · SYDNEY

Our thanks to: Anton Mueller and the team at Bloomsbury; design assistants Matt Brimicombe and Martha Barry; research assistant Eli Battles; Lawry Hutcheson, who helped us build a rocket launcher; and Matt Glenn and Megan Folz, who helped us build a cornhole set. We are particularly grateful to our children: Sam and Max Glenn; Peter, Henrik, and Luisa Schleisman; and Luciano and Luna Leone.

This book would not have been possible without the assistance of the following gamers, young and old: Jon Pinchera; Michael Keller; Adam Banks; Rhett, Patty, Cole, and Josie Johnson; James, Sacha, Riley, and Jackson Walser; Lee Glenn and Sandra Roe; Catherine Hooley; John Robinson, P.E. teacher at the Learning Project (Boston, Mass.); and the staff at Camp Widjiwagan (Ely, Minn.). We also want to give a shout-out to the following stores, which are staffed by enthusiastic game geeks: The Compleat Strategist (Boston, Mass.), Eureka Puzzles (Brookline, Mass.), and JP Comics and Games (Boston, Mass.).

Published by Bloomsbury USA, New York

Bloomsbury is a trademark of Bloomsbury Publishing Plc

All papers used by Bloomsbury USA are natural, recyclable products made from wood grown in well-managed forests. The manufacturing processes conform to the environmental regulations of the country of origin.

LIBRARY OF CONGRESS CATALOGING-IN-PUBLICATION DATA HAS BEEN APPLIED FOR

ISBN: 978-1-62040-706-6

First U.S. Edition 2014

1 3 5 7 9 10 8 6 4 2

Design and Art Direction by Tony Leone, Leone Design
Design assistance by Matt Brimicombe and Martha Barry
Illustration illumination by Matt Brimicombe and Tony Leone

Cover design by Tony Leone
Cover illustration by Mister Reusch

For more activities and info, visit our website: Unbored.net

Printed and bound in China by C&C Offset Printing Co. Ltd

Bloomsbury books may be purchased for business or promotional use. For information on bulk purchases please contact Macmillan Corporate and Premium Sales Department at specialmarkets@macmillan.com.

DISCLAIMER

The information contained in this book is for informational and entertainment purposes only. We have done our best to be as factual and accurate as possible, but we do not guarantee that any of the information contained in this book is correct or workable. Be responsible, exercise good sense, and take every safety precaution—not limited to the precautions that we suggest. Also, we do not advocate the breaking of any law.

Note that when following our instructions, switching materials, assembling improperly, mishandling and misusing can cause harm; also, results may vary.

It is important that you understand that the authors, the publisher, and the bookseller cannot and will not guarantee your safety. Physical or mental harm is not intended so be cautious and use at your own risk. The authors and publishers expressly disclaim liability for any injury or damages resulting from the use (proper or otherwise) of any information in this book.

RECIPES, FORMULAS, ACTIVITIES, AND INSTRUCTIONS IN THIS BOOK SHOULD BE FOLLOWED EXACTLY AND SHOULD NOT BE ATTEMPTED WITHOUT ADULT SUPERVISION.

Because of the Children's Online Privacy Protection Act (COPPA), most major websites are restricted to users 13 and older. We do not advocate lying about your age in order to access websites, games, apps, social media services, and anything else online mentioned or not mentioned in this book. Parents should not help their children lie about their age online; if underage children make use of email, instant messaging, Facebook, YouTube, Twitter, or any other website, game, app, or social media service, including web searches, they should only do so via a parent's account and with close parental supervision and collaboration.

While the authors have made every effort to provide accurate internet addresses at the time of publication, neither the publisher nor the authors assume any responsibility for errors, or for changes that occur after publication. Further, the publisher does not have any control over and does not assume any responsibility for author or third-party websites or their content.

chapter 1 PWNAGE

Chapter 2
HOME GAMES

Chapter 3
GAME CHANGERS

Chapter 4
ADVENTURE GAMES

UNBORED'S
GAME ON!
MANIFESTO

By Josh and Elizabeth

Here's our Top 10 list of reasons for kids and grownups to take games— from boardgames to active outdoor games to videogames—seriously.

1 Gaming encourages you to develop skills and expertise, by practicing something over and over. More importantly, gaming challenges you to *teach yourself* how to do something.

2 Although we live in a "throwaway" culture, gaming is all about hacking, modifying, and improving stuff you already own. If you don't like the way a game works, instead of tossing it out you can make it work better.

3 Active games not only help you improve your coordination and develop agility and flexibility, but they also build self-confidence. There is no more enjoyable way to get and stay fit than to run around playing a game.

4 Games exercise your imagination and develop your problem-solving skills. Plus, playing games encourages you to hack, modify, and improve your own mindset and behavior.

5 Gaming makes you resilient and determined; you have to develop "grit." Why bother? Because developing grit helps you to become independent. Gaming teaches you to actually do what you say you're going to do.

6 What are you really good at? What motivates you? What makes you happy? Gaming teaches you the answers to these important questions: not just who you are, but what makes you tick.

7 Gaming teaches you that your environment is modifiable. You realize that everyday life is a puzzle to be solved: the more difficult the obstacles, the more fun you'll have figuring out how to beat them.

8 Sharing games with others—teaching and learning the best strategies—is very rewarding. Whether you win or lose the game doesn't matter, because although gaming is competitive, playing a game is always a collaboration.

9 Jumping in and making mistakes is the fastest way to learn how to play a game. Not worrying about being perfect, and just trying your best, is known as "fun failure."

10 Each time you play a game, you enter a world in which grownups aren't in control. When it comes to games, there are no teachers or coaches—it's up to you, with a little help from your friends.

Illustration by Mister Reusch

THINK LIKE
A GAMER!

By Chris Dahlen

"Follow the rules" sounds like an order. But if you're a gamer, you know that a game's rules pose an exciting challenge: What can I do within these limits that nobody has done before?

The following gamer's guidelines apply to every sort of game—including life itself.

Learn the Rules

When you're young and everything's blurry and shapeless, your first job is to discover the rules. An adult hides behind his own pair of hands, and then he springs out and shouts, "Peek-a-boo!" You laugh, and then he does it again. After a while, you realize that the joke here is that he does it the same way every time—that the hiding precedes the peeking and booing. Running through the grass screaming is fun, but it's not a game. If you add a simple set of rules to your play—first, hide; then, shout "Peek-a-boo!"—you get a new kind of fun. A game called Peek-a-boo.

Enforce the Rules

On the playground, a PE teacher might lay down the laws of various games: "That's against the rules," or "Here's how you play Four Square." But kids can teach each other the rules, too, by telling each other how to survive a game of dodgeball, say, or win at *Scrabble* by always going for triple letter scores. Even with a game as complicated as baseball, most kids don't sit down and read a rulebook—they learn it as they go. When the baseball coach isn't there, the players keep each other in line.

If you're a gamer, then you never break a game's rules. Instead, you try to play the game—within the rules—your way. You learn which tactics work well

Illustrations by Mister Reusch

and then, just when others think they have you figured out, you switch everything up and surprise them. You keep a straight face when you're holding a winning hand of cards (or a losing one, for that matter).

The better that you get at playing a game—whether it's soccer or *Apples to Apples* or two-player *Skylanders*—the more important it becomes to enforce the rules. If you break the rules, you break the game. But stick to them, and you can win fair and square! There's no more satisfying feeling.

Modify the Rules

Although gamers don't break a game's rules, they know there's nothing wrong with modifying the game—sometimes to the point where it becomes a new game. If you've ever lowered a basketball net to

GAMES
MY SON & I PLAY
By Chris Dahlen

Machinarium
machinarium.net
The first game we ever played. We sat side-by-side at the computer, helping a robot save his friends and his city.

Eets Munchies
eetsgame.com
A charming 2-D puzzle game that challenges us both. I swear my kid is the one who keeps hitting the "Hint" button, not me.

Portal 2
thinkwithportals.com
This clever puzzle game casts us as two slapstick robots who are forced to work together—and I mean really cooperate—in order to solve a series of challenges. You can also just knock each other's heads off.

The Adventures of Kodu
The first game that my kid ever designed, using Microsoft's Kodu platform (soon to be supplanted by Project Spark). I'm even prouder of the game than he is.

Skylanders
skylanders.com
I'm too old for toys. But this franchise, which crosses physical figures with video games, gives us a chance to play with action figures.

Android: Netrunner
This high-stakes two-player card game was designed for adults. So why does my kid beat me every time?

Rayman Origins and Rayman Legends
ubi.com
Michel Ancel's platformers make you feel like you're living in a cartoon. It's easy to get in each other's way with two players, but the wonder and humor make it worthwhile.

Spelunky
spelunkyworld.com
An Indiana Jones-style adventure that changes every time you play it. This game will tax your skills and test your endurance—especially when your "partner" knocks you into a spike trap.

Papo y Yo
weareminority.com
The game tells the story of the troubled relationship that game designer Vander Caballero had growing up with his father, who is portrayed here as a monster with a terrible temper. Sure, it felt strange to play it with my own son. But we don't always get along—or play well together.

Frisbee
Whenever we get fed up with each other, we go outside and just throw a frisbee until we both cool down. It never fails.

help smaller kids compete, or changed the "house rules" in *Monopoly* to share the wealth from the Free Parking space, or used the specialized dice or figures that came with one game in order to create a completely different game, then you're a gamer. A few years ago, someone invented a version of Tic-Tac-Toe where you're playing on nine grids at once; with that one simple change, a boring game for little kids became interesting again.

Pay attention to how your fellow players act, react, struggle, fight, and have fun. Game designers do this all the time, when they're "playtesting" a new game. If the rules feel too easy, a gamer tightens them up; if they're too frustrating, a gamer gives people new options.

Rewrite the Rules

A gamer understands that when a game's rules aren't working, cheating or quitting doesn't help. If the rules aren't fair—when the same person or team wins the game every single time—then stop everything and write new rules. The game of chess has changed over the centuries; so has the Constitution of the United States.

The rules that we take for granted in everyday life—about how to wait in line, for example—were invented at some point in the past. A gamer understands that it's important to follow these rules when they're fair, and when they make life enjoyable and rewarding. But a gamer also understands that sometimes life's rules need to be modified, even rewritten.

As a gamer, you already know how to step up and demonstrate a better way. Whether in your backyard, on the school playground, or in life generally, think hard about the rules of the game, and propose changes to the unfair ones. If you can convince others to agree with your new rules, then everyone can come out a winner.

It's on you to change rules that don't make sense

BEST EVER

QUICK BOARDGAMES

When it comes to playing boardgames on a typical weeknight, most families don't have more than 45 minutes to spare. So here's an all-time favorite list of several fast-paced, seriously entertaining boardgames.

Apples to Apples

Designed by Matthew Kirby and Mark Alan Osterhaus

Each player is dealt a hand of Description cards, each of which features a single word: "Glamorous," for example, or "Ridiculous" or "Messy" or "Cool." The player taking a turn as the game's referee picks a Thing card (e.g., "Arnold Schwarzenegger," "Poodles," "My Room"), and the other players try to find the description best matching that thing in their own hand. There's a lot of arguing and other efforts to persuade the referee, but it's all in good fun.

Players: 4–10 | **Age:** 9+
Duration: 30 minutes

Party Playoff

Designed by Kim Vandenbroucke

Before this voting game begins, 32 "contenders"—e.g., Campsite, Cookie Monster, Skiing, Frisbee—are drawn from a pool of several hundred possibilities, and placed on a NCAA-type tournament bracket in one of four categories: Places, People, Actions, Things. Then you create match-ups—Cookie Monster vs. Beyoncé, say—and vote on questions like, "With whom would you rather be stuck in an elevator?" It's absurd and hilarious.

Players: 4+ | **Age:** 8+
Duration: 30 minutes

Ghost Blitz
(aka Geistesblitz)

Designed by Jacques Zeimet

There are five little objects on the table. A card depicting two of the objects is flipped over, after which one of two things happens. If one object on the card is colored incorrectly, then the first player to grab the correctly colored object wins. However, if both objects on the card are colored incorrectly, then the first player to grab the only object whose shape and color is *not* represented on the card wins.

Players: 2–8 | **Age:** 8+
Duration: 20 minutes

Ticket to Ride

Designed by Alan R. Moon

The board is an old-fashioned map—e.g., of North America, Europe, or elsewhere, depending on which edition of the game you're using. Players are issued colored train pieces, and dealt train-car cards; they're also dealt destination tickets, each of which shows a pair of cities on the map that you must sneakily attempt to connect… by claiming railroad routes. Longer routes are worth more points than shorter routes, but are trickier to claim.

Players: 2–5 | **Age:** 8+
Duration: 45 minutes

Memoir '44

Designed by Richard Borg

Create a scenario representing one of World War II's most famous battles—e.g., Omaha Beach, Pegasus Bridge, Operation Cobra—and then duke it out with an opponent by deploying infantry, paratrooper, tank, and artillery units, not to mention resistance fighters. The miniature figures are highly detailed, the strategy is absorbing, and the rules are simple enough that even some 6-year-olds of our acquaintance enjoy playing this game.

Players: 2 | **Age:** 8+
Duration: 60 minutes

Anomia

Designed by Andrew Innes

The name means "a problem remembering a word," and that's exactly the point of this game. On your turn, you flip over a card featuring both a symbol and a word representing a category—e.g., "Color," "Fairy Tale," "Mountain." If the symbol on your card matches the symbol on another player's card, then the two of you must race to name an example of that category—e.g., "Red," "Hansel and Gretel," "Everest." Easy, right? Not when your adrenaline is pumping.

Players: 3–6 | **Age:** 10+
Duration: 20 minutes

MEMOIR '44
HACKS

By Tony Leone

My son, Luciano, and I enjoy the expansion packs for the WWII boardgame *Memoir '44*. But it's more fun to hack (customize) the game yourself. So try these tips, and let the battle begin!

Recruit Unique Troops

Want to add paratroopers, engineers, or mountain troops to the game? We've picked up 1:72 scale WWII figures—Airfix and Revell make good ones—online, and at our local hobby shop. Because they look cooler than the game's standard troops, we designate our unique troops as elite units.

If you add infantry carrying mortars to your game, then you should make their range of fire longer than normal. And if you add combat engineers (they carry pickaxes, shovels, and mine sweepers), then you'll need rules about building bridges—e.g., in order to build a new bridge, the engineer unit must occupy a hex adjacent to a river for 5 turns.

Add combat engineers who can build (and blow up) bridges. Repurpose Lego dynamite pieces to set the charge.

Photos by Tony Leone

Dungeon Roll

Designed by Chris Darden
In this press-your-luck dice game, each player is a Hero (e.g., a Bard, or an Enchantress) leading a team of adventurers on a "dungeon delve." On your turn, you'll collect as many experience points as possible—by fighting monsters, gathering treasure, and perhaps even facing a dragon—while strategizing about future delves. Should you use your Thief to open a treasure chest, or save him to fight a dragon? Whoever scores the most, wins.

Players: 1–4 | **Age:** 8+
Duration: 15 minutes

Blokus

Designed by Bernard Tavitian
Each player has a set of 21 tiles, which come in lots of shapes; on each turn, you place one of your tiles on the board in such a fashion that it touches one of your own pieces (at a corner only) and simultaneously blocks off as much of the board for yourself as possible. Because playing this tile-placement game (pronounced "block-us") is sort of like doing a jigsaw puzzle with friends, you might find yourself accidentally offering helpful tips to opponents. Oops!

Players: 2–4 | **Age:** 5+
Duration: 20 minutes

Carcassonne

Designed by Klaus-Jürgen Wrede
In this tile-placement game, players take turns adding to a landscape map of a medieval civilization. After placing each new tile, you may station a "meeple" (boardgamer slang for a person-shaped playing piece) on that tile. The goal is to control the longest roads, the largest cities, and the most advantageously sited farms. Play is fast, and no player is ever eliminated.

Players: 2–5 | **Age:** 8+
Duration: 45 minutes

Capture the Commander

Memoir '44 doesn't come with commanders—that is, figures with binoculars, field phones, or walkie talkies. But if you add a 1:72 scale commander figure to your game, then you can play "Capture the Commander." We add a commander figure to an elite infantry unit; if this "command unit" is knocked out by your opponent, then you automatically lose the game.

Blow Stuff Up

Some *Memoir '44* expansion packs come with mines, but Luciano invented a minefield rule that we prefer. Draw skulls on slips of paper, and hide them under terrain hexes. When your opponent moves a unit onto a mined hex, yell, "Mines!" Your opponent loses one member of that unit, and the minefield is revealed. If the attackers are engineers, they disarm the mines.

Add an element of surprise—hide mines!

Here's another explosive scenario. We place a Lego dynamite piece on a bridge, with a victory medal (the attacking player's objective) on the other side of the river. If the defending player can keep the attackers off the bridge for 10 turns (say), then the bridge blows up. But if the attacker captures the bridge before 10 turns have passed, then the dynamite is disarmed.

WHO'S IT?

The counter

When you're playing Tag or Hide-and-Seek, how do you select who's "It"? The most fun way is to turn the choosing process itself into a game.

Spuds Up

Everyone stands in a circle and puts both fists ("spuds," an old slang word for potatoes) forward. The counter chants:

> One potato, two potato,
> three potato, four.
> Five potato, six potato,
> seven potato, more.

The counter
uses her chin
as a "potato"

While naming each potato, the counter moves her fist around the circle, tapping each player's spuds; when she gets around to herself, she taps her own chin, then taps the fist that she's not using for counting-out. Whichever spud she's tapping when the counter gets to the word "more" is eliminated—so that player puts his spud behind his back. (If the counter's chin is out, she doesn't tap it the next time around.) Then she starts the rhyme again, beginning with the next spud.

When a player's two spuds are out, he leaves the circle. The game continues until there is only one spud left—and that player is It.

Illustrations by Mister Reusch

More rhymes

You can make up your own counting-out rhymes, or try some of the ones that we've collected.

Ink-a-dink
A bottle of ink
Cork fell out
And you stink.

Superman, Superman fly
    away
Superman, Superman
    save the day.

Skunk in the barnyard,
    pee-yew!
Somebody farted, that's
    you.

More counting-out games

Tarzan, Tarzan, in a tree
How many gallons did he
    pee?

Bubblegum, bubblegum,
    in a dish
How many pieces do you
    wish?

If the counter was pointing to you when she got to "pee" or "wish," you say a number between 1 and 10. Then the counter points around the circle while counting, and whichever person she ends up on is not It.

Engine, Engine
    Number Nine
Going down Chicago
    line
If the train goes off
    the track
Do you want your
    money back?

If the counter was pointing to you when she got to "back," you say "Yes" or "No." Then the counter spells out Y-E-S or N-O, and whoever "gets" the last letter is not It.

My mother and your
    mother were hanging
    up clothes
My mother punched your
    mother right in the
    nose
What color was the blood?

HISTORICAL COUNTING-OUT GAMES

Wee-Wo, Wack

In the early 19th century, children used the following rhyme:

Hannah, Man, Mona,
    Mike
Barcelona, Bono, Strike
Hare, Ware, Frown,
    Vanack
Harrico, Warico,
    Wee-Wo, Wack.

The last player with a spud in the game is It

The counter then spells out whichever color was chosen. Whichever person "gets" the last letter of the word is not It.

One spot, two spot

In the 1933 Marx Brothers movie *Duck Soup*, which your grownups should show you right away, the following counting-out rhyme is used:

One spot, two spot,
    zig-zag, tear
Pop-die, pennygot,
    tennyum, tear
Harum-scarum, rip'em,
    tear'em
Tay, taw, toe.

BACK OF THE
CLASSROOM

Players: 2

When you're bored—on car trips, in doctor's waiting rooms, and even in the back of the classroom—try playing these games.

CIRCLE-HAND

According to legend, the Circle-Hand Game (also called the Hole-Tempting Game) was invented in the 1920s by students at the City College of New York. We also hear that every submarine crew plays this game—which makes sense, because they must get pretty bored.

Using your thumb and forefinger, make the "OK" sign, otherwise known as a circle. If you can trick a friend into looking directly at your circle-hand, you score a point. But if they only look at it out of the

corner of their eye and can poke their finger into the circle-hand, then they score a point. However, if you trap their finger in your circle-hand, you score 10 points.

One common rule is that you must not raise your circle-hand above your waist; a less strict variation allows you to place your circle-hand anywhere—except not directly in front of someone's face.

➡ HACKS

- Make a circle-hand, and don't say anything to your intended victim; even if she knows what you're doing, eventually she won't be able to help herself—she'll look.

- Make a circle-hand, then say something like, "Oh! What's this I found in my pocket?" Or: "Hey, is this yours?" Or: "Does this belong to you?"

COIN HOCKEY

You'll need three coins of the same size, the larger the better. Sit facing your opponent across a table.

Defense

1. The defending player forms a goal by placing her palms on the edge of the table with the tips of her stretched-out thumbs touching; or, sometimes, by placing her fists against the edge of the table, with her pinkies extended.

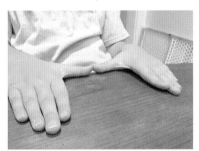

Which style of goal do you prefer? Kids have debated this question for generations.

Offense

1. The player on offense forms the coins into a triangle, with one coin near his edge of the table, and the other two coins in front of that one.

2. The offensive player then taps sharply downward on the first coin, sending the other two sliding across the table; flicking is also OK.

3. Then, the offensive player chooses one of the three coins and tries to tap it so that it slides between the other two coins without touching them.

4. He repeats this until he's able to tap a coin into the goal—one point! If he hits one of the coins with the tapped coin, or hits a coin off the table, or isn't able to slide a coin between the other two coins, then it's the other player's turn.

PAPER FOOTBALL

First, you need to make a football. You'll need an 8½x11" sheet of paper.

Make the football

1. Fold the sheet of paper in half, lengthwise, twice.

2. With the paper oriented vertically in front of you, fold the lower right corner diagonally up and to the left, forming a triangle shape. Now fold straight up, so the strip's bottom edge is straight across again. Next, fold the lower left corner diagonally up and to the right, forming another triangle shape. Continue until you reach the top.

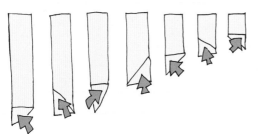

4. Finally, fold the top edge's corners down (to make it more tuck-able); then tuck the top edge down into the football's final fold.

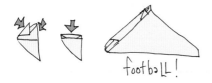

football!

The field and the rules

- Now that you have a football, you'll need a field; any table top will do, though rectangular ones are the most football-field-like.

- The team with the ball advances down the field by flicking the football, either with a thumb or finger, down the field. You only get one flick per turn; if the ball stops with any part of it sticking out over the far edge of the table, it's a touchdown—6 points!

- If the ball goes off the side of the table, it's placed back on the table at the approximate "yard line" where it went off.

- If the ball stops short of the far edge of the table, then you make a field goal attempt: use a finger from one hand to hold the football vertically, and use a finger from your other hand to flick the ball into the air and through the goal posts. (What goal posts? The defending player forms goal posts by touching the tips of her stretched-out thumbs together, and pointing her fingers straight up in the air. Please note that you do not want to flick the football into someone's eye!) If the field goal is successful, you score 3 points.

- It can also be fun to play a version of the game where you just kick field goals back and forth.

you'll draw both armies—but if it's a two-player game, then each player can draw his or her own army.

2. On your turn, spend no more than five seconds studying the battlefield. Memorize the position of one enemy unit that you want to target. Then flip the paper over, and gently punch the pencil through the blank side—at the position where you believe the targeted unit is. Flip the paper over to the battlefield side again, and see if you scored a hit on an enemy unit.

3. Take turns punching the pencil through the blank side of the paper until one army has lost all its units. If the person who played first is the winner, then the other player gets one last try.

KER-PUNCH

You'll need:

- A pencil
- A sheet of paper—one that you can't easily see through

Try this:

1. Draw two armies, each composed of the same number of individual units, on the same side of the paper. The units in each army should be approximately the same size, and they should all look alike: For example, the units in army "A" might be wearing helmets, while the units in army "B" are not. (Stick figures are OK!) To make the game easier, draw the units in army "A" on the left side of the page, and the units in army "B" on the right; to make the game more challenging, mix the two armies up on the page. If you're playing Ker-punch solo, then

➡ HACKS

- Try "salvo" mode. Each player, on her turn, punches as many holes as she has units left; in other words, if you have three units left, then you get to punch three holes.

- Vary the battle scenario. Draw an army of aliens vs. an army of Earthlings; or two armies of underwater commandoes; or Redcoats vs. Minutemen; or monsters vs. mice.

- For a nonviolent version of the game, draw two "armies" of lettuce and carrots. Now you're rabbits, competing to steal vegetables from a garden. Ker-munch! (Thanks, Robin and Juniper, for the idea.)

BIKE
RODEO

Players: 2+

Although they're associated with the American and Canadian West, rodeos started as a way for Spanish and Mexican cowboys to show off the skills they needed to drive cattle. Today, they are rough and wild contests that are as adrenaline-filled as any X Games event.

They're also controversial, due to concerns that the animals in the events aren't treated humanely. A bike rodeo is a more humane option that's still a freewheeling test of agility, speed, and endurance.

You'll need:
- Bikes
- Bike helmets (duh)
- 15 traffic cones or other markers (bean bags, masking or duct tape also work)
- A phone stopwatch
- Measuring tape
- Sidewalk chalk
- 5 laundry baskets, large boxes, or trash pails
- 5 newspapers or magazines, rolled up and secured with rubber bands
- A messenger bag
- Large cement surface (an empty parking lot works well)
- **Optional:** Knee and elbow pads

Slalom
Place 13 markers in a long straight line, with each marker 4' apart from the next. Then place 1 marker 30' from the first marker and another marker 10' after the last; these are your start and finish lines. Appoint someone to time how long it takes each rider to race from the start line to the finish line, weaving in and out of the markers. Hitting or knocking over a marker adds 5 seconds to a rider's time; or, if you prefer, it disqualifies that ride.

Illustrations by Mister Reusch

Coaster

Using chalk, mark a starting line. Then mark a second line 25' away. Taking turns, each rider must pedal like crazy from the first line to the second, taking her feet off the pedals as she crosses the second line. Mark how far each rider can coast past the second line.

➡ **HACKS**

- Do these courses on inline skates, a scooter, or a skateboard.
- Add ramps to the start and finish lines.

Figure 8

Place 14 cones in the shape of a 60-foot "figure 8," leaving 2' of space between the top and bottom circles. Time how fast someone can complete the entire figure-8 loop—riding just outside the markers—three times. Hitting or knocking over a marker adds five seconds to a rider's time. In this case, note that the starting line is also the finish line.

Paper carrier

Using chalk, draw a course for riders to follow. At different points along the course, and several feet away from the actual course, place the five baskets. On your turn, you will don a messenger bag containing the five rolled-up newspapers sticking out the top of the bag for easy access. Ride the course as fast as you can, trying to throw a newspaper into each basket. Each correct toss is 10 points.

PS: If you are allowed to ride around your neighborhood, you can chart out a much bigger game—and even put the baskets in more difficult places, including the low boughs of a pine tree or on the roof of your grownup's car.

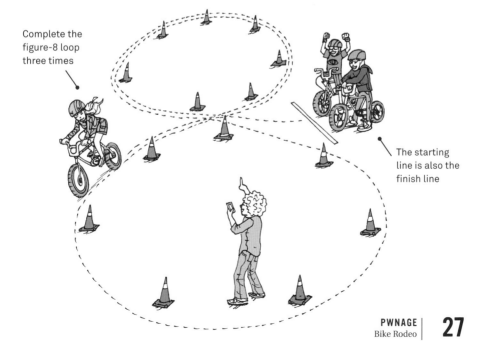

Complete the figure-8 loop three times

The starting line is also the finish line

HISTORY'S ROUGHEST GAMES

If you think rodeos are out of control, take a look at these cruel events from ancient history.

Ancient Romans enjoyed watching gladiators battle in amphitheaters like the Colosseum

Mesoamerican ballgame

The oldest known sport in the Americas, the Mesoamerican ballgame was first played over 3700 years ago in southern Mexico and was an important event for the Maya, Olmec, Zapotec, and Aztec cultures. Played in open-air grass ball-courts surrounded by massive stone walls, the most popular version of the game involved players of two teams using nothing but their hips to score by getting a rubber ball into the opposing team's end zone.

The Mesoamerican ballgame was extremely violent and dangerous. Players wore leather pads to protect themselves, but these didn't make much of a difference if your team didn't win since losers were often decapitated. Talk about having a lot on the line!

While experts aren't exactly sure how this game got its start, they suspect the ball players were noblemen who were trying to get richer and more powerful—by killing their rivals.

FUN FACT: Played today in the Mexican state of Sinaloa, *Ulama* is a fun, non-lethal version of the original ballgame.

Gladiator games

Between 1800 and 2100 years ago, it was all the rage for Romans to spend a pleasant afternoon watching gladiators (*gladius* means sword in Latin) fighting for their lives against wild animals, condemned criminals, and other gladiators. They were often criminals who had no choice but to compete. Legend has it that the fate of the losing gladiator was chosen by the crowd: Thumbs-up meant that his life was spared; thumbs-down meant he was a goner.

Gladiator games took place in amphitheaters, which are oval-shaped buildings that look a lot like football stadiums. The most famous Roman amphitheater that you can still visit is the Colosseum in Rome.

Illustration by Mister Reusch

DAIFUGO

Daifugo

Fugo

Hinmin

Daihinmin

Players: 4+

This Japanese card game has become popular in the West under a variety of names—including (in the United States) President, The Great Dalmuti, and Capitalism.

You'll need:
• A standard 52-card deck of playing cards

Try this:

1. The object of Daifugo is to run out of cards first. Whoever succeeds in doing so is the Daifugo (or Extremely Wealthy). Whoever runs out second is the Fugo (Wealthy). Whoever runs out last is the Daihinmin (Extremely Broke); second-to-last is the Hinmin (Broke).

2. To start the game, the Daihinmin (the previous round's loser) deals all the cards. Note: If this is the game's first round, then the players decide randomly who will be the dealer.

3. Arrange your cards in rank order, from highest to lowest: 2 − A − K − Q − J − 10 − 9 − 8 − 7 − 6 − 5 − 4 − 3. Yes, the highest-ranking card is the 2.

fugo

Play proceeds clockwise

daifugo

hinmin

The Daihinmin is the dealer

daihinmin

4. Taxation time! The Daihinmin must hand over his two strongest cards to the Daifugo; the Daifugo gives back two cards he doesn't want. And the Hinmin must hand over his strongest card to the Fugo; the Fugo hands back one card. If this is the first round, skip the taxation.

5. During each of the round's various tricks, the Daifugo (who should be sitting on the dealer's left) leads—by playing between one and four cards of the same rank. Play then proceeds clockwise. The number of cards you play on your turn isn't up to you; it's up to the Daifugo. If he plays two cards when starting a trick, then everyone else must play two cards during that trick. If he plays one card, then everyone else must play one card. And so forth.

Exception: The 2 is so powerful that you may never play more than one 2 card. When a 2 is played, the trick immediately ends—and the person who played the 2 leads the next trick.

6. Another important rule: Each player must play cards of a higher rank than the cards played by the preceding player! So if the first player plays three Kings, for example, then the second player can only take her turn if she can play either three Aces or a single 2. If she does play three Aces, then the next player can only take his turn if he has a 2 to play.

7. Can't—or don't choose to—play, when your turn comes around? Knock on the table, in order to signal that you're passing your turn to the next player. Or you can just say "Pass."

8. Play continues until all players pass, or until one or more 2's are played. (Nothing can beat 2's.) As mentioned, whoever plays the last card of a trick gets to play first during that round's next trick.

9. Tricks continue until one player runs out of cards. He is now out of play—and will be the Daifugo in the following round. However, the round continues without that player, until the game's other titles (first Fugo, then Hinmin, then Daihinmin) have been determined as well.

10. When the round ends, players must then switch seats so that the Daifugo (that round's winner) is to the left of the Daihinmin (that round's loser), and everyone else is seated clockwise to the left of the Daifugo in order of their rank. The Hinmin must always be seated to the Daihinmin's right.

⇒ **HACKS** - - - - - - - -

At the beginning of each new round, the new Daifugo is allowed to make up a rule—e.g., "One-eyed Jacks are wild cards"—which governs that round's (and only that round's) play.

MINDGAME

The Only...
STATES

The 50 states that make up the United States of America are a source of fascinating facts and figures. More turkeys are raised in California than in any other state. The first Kentucky Fried Chicken restaurant was opened in Utah in 1952. And Texas is home to more species of bat than anywhere else in the US. But flying creatures aren't the only interesting thing about our federation. If you're a word nerd, you'll appreciate the verbal variety on display across all of the state names.

To which end, can you identify the following six states from their unique linguistic DNA?

1. What is the only state that contains three Cs?
2. What is the only state that contains the letter Z?
3. What is the only state that contains four As?
4. What is the only state that contains two As and two Es?
5. What is the only state that contains only one consonant and has no repeating letters?
6. What is the only state that contains two Ps?

THE JEWEL GAME

AN EXCERPT FROM

KIM

by Rudyard Kipling

Rudyard Kipling is best known as author of *The Jungle Book*. When the titular hero of Kipling's 1901 novel *Kim*, an orphaned boy living by his wits in India, is recruited as an agent by the British secret service, the Hindu jeweler and spymaster Mr. Lurgan trains him to memorize details quickly and accurately. How? By means of a Concentration-type game that uses jewels and other objects as game pieces.

From a drawer under the table [Lurgan] dealt a half-handful of clattering trifles into the tray.

"Now," said [Lurgan's son], waving an old newspaper. "Look on them as long as thou wilt, stranger. Count and, if need be, handle. One look is enough for me." He turned his back proudly.

"But what is the game?"

"When thou hast counted and handled and art sure that thou canst remember them all, I cover them with this paper, and thou must tell over the tally to Lurgan Sahib. I will write mine."

"Oah!" The instinct of competition waked in [Kim's] breast. He bent over the tray. There were but fifteen stones on it. "That is easy," he said after a minute. The child slipped the paper over the winking jewels and scribbled in a native account-book.

"There are under that paper five blue stones—one big, one smaller, and three small," said Kim, all in haste. "There are four green stones, and one with a hole in it; there is one yellow stone that I can see through, and one like a pipe-stem. There are two red stones, and—and—I made the count fifteen, but two I have forgotten. No! Give me time. One was of ivory, little and brownish; and—and—give me time…"

"One—two"—Lurgan Sahib counted him out up to ten. Kim shook his head.

"Hear my count!" the child burst in, trilling with laughter. "First, are two flawed sapphires—one of two ruttees and one of four as I should judge. The four-ruttee sapphire is chipped at the edge. There is one Turkestan turquoise, plain with black veins, and there are two inscribed—one with a Name of God in gilt, and the other being cracked across, for it came out of an old ring, I cannot read. We have now all five blue stones. Four flawed emeralds there are, but one is drilled in two places, and one is a little carven—"

"Their weights?" said Lurgan Sahib impassively.

"Three—five—five—and four ruttees as I judge it. There is one piece of old greenish pipe amber, and a cut topaz from Europe. There is one ruby of Burma, of two ruttees, without a flaw, and there is a balas-ruby, flawed, of two ruttees. There is a carved ivory from China representing a rat sucking an egg; and there is last—ah ha!—a ball of crystal as big as a bean set on a gold leaf."

He clapped his hands at the close.

"He is thy master," said Lurgan Sahib, smiling.

"Huh! He knew the names of the stones," said Kim, flushing. "Try again! With common things such as he and I both know."

They heaped the tray again with odds and ends gathered from the shop, and even the kitchen, and every time the child won, till Kim marvelled.

"Bind my eyes—let me feel once with my fingers, and even then I will leave thee opened-eyed behind," he challenged.

Kim stamped with vexation when the lad made his boast good.

"If it were men—or horses," he said, "I could do better. This playing with tweezers and knives and scissors is too little."

"Learn first—teach later," said Lurgan Sahib.

HIGHLAND GAMES

A thousand years ago in Scotland, the Celts competed in a war-like series of competitions known as the Highland Games. Some speculate that clan chieftains invented the games as a way to choose the strongest, bravest, and fastest warriors, couriers, and bodyguards.

Versions of these competitions still take place in Scotland and elsewhere, only now they're just for fun. In addition to kilts, dancing, and bagpipe action, the Highland Games are known for the following "heavy" events, *which you should definitely not try at home.*

Caber Toss

Competitors carry a tall (nearly 20') wooden pole and "toss" it. The pole (usually a log) can weigh 175 pounds, so just picking it up results in a lot of knee buckling and staggering around the field. Plus, when you throw it, the pole is supposed to flip over 180 degrees.

Sheaf Toss

Using a pitchfork, competitors spear a 16-lb. burlap sack stuffed with straw—and hurl it over a bar, which is usually set higher than their heads. If your sack clears it, then the bar is raised. Whoever tosses the sack of straw over the highest bar wins.

Illustrations by Mister Reusch

Here are a couple of Highland Games-style competitions that you *can* try at home.

TUG-OF-WAR

Players: 6+

You'll need:

- A large open area, at the center of which is a mud pit, wading pool—or a marker (e.g., a soft traffic cone, somebody's sweatshirt) than won't hurt if you fall onto it.
- A strong, 120' length of rope (preferably nylon, to reduce rope-burn). If you're playing with younger kids, use rope no thicker than 1" so they can easily grip it.
- A bandana or rag
- A roll of brightly colored duct tape
- **Optional:** A referee

Try this:

1. Divide into two equally strong teams (which might mean, e.g., one grownup vs. three kids).

2. Match the center point of the rope to the center spot on the tug-of-war playing field, and lay the rope down. Uncoil it in a straight line.

3. Tie a rag or bandana at the rope's mid-point. Measure 15' in either direction from the rope's center, and mark these points on the rope with duct tape. Then measure another 2' away from these marks (towards the ends of the rope) and make another set of marks, You're not allowed to hold the rope any closer to its center than these second marks!

4. The teams should now line up along the rope—standing behind the marked spots. Arrange yourselves strategically: Often, the strongest team member serves as the "anchor" (at the end of the rope).

5. Next, everybody picks up the rope and makes sure that its center mark is exactly above the playing field's mud pit, cone, or whatever you're using. This is where a referee is useful.

6. Pull! When one team's first duct-tape mark crosses the field's center, the other team wins.

Tie a rag at the rope's mid-point

15'

15'

2'

Mark the center spot of the tug-of-war playing field

HAMMER TOSS

Players: 2+

You'll need:

- A large open area
- A 3-foot section of PVC pipe or bamboo pole
- Heavy-duty duct tape
- A block of styrofoam, approximately 8"x6"x4" (really, any size will work). You can buy styrofoam (or any kind of hard foam) at craft stores and moving stores.
- A short length of rope—3' long will do
- Measuring tape

Get into the spirit of the Highland Games by wearing a kilt!

Make the hammer:

1. Poke the end of the pipe or pole firmly into the center of the styrofoam.

2. Wrap the entire styrofoam block with duct tape, using the tape to secure the block (the hammer's head) to the pipe or pole (the hammer's shaft). Your hammer is ready to toss!

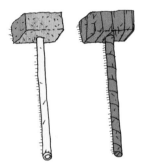

Play the game:

1. At one end of your hammer-toss field, use the rope to create a line.

2. The first competitor stands behind the line, holding the hammer. Toss the hammer as far as you can, without stepping over the line. (Any method you choose is OK. The Scots stand backwards—facing away from the line—and twirl the hammer above their heads before letting it sail. Check it out on YouTube.) Using the tape measure, measure the distance between the line and the hammer.

3. Each competitor takes a turn. Whoever throws the hammer the longest distance wins.

HOT
DICE

Players: 2+

Hot Dice, also sometimes known as Greed, Squelch, Zilch, or Farkle, is a folk game, which means that no one knows who invented it... or the "true" rules. Here are the rules that we use.

You'll need:

- 6 six-sided dice
- Paper and pencil, for keeping score

Try this:

1. The goal of Hot Dice is to score 10,000 points.

2. Each 1 that you throw is worth 100 points; and each 5 is worth 50.

    Three of a kind is scored as follows: three 1's = 1,000, three 6's = 600, three 5's = 500, three 4's = 400, three 3's = 300 pts, three 2's = 200.

    If you roll four of a kind, you add 1,000 points to your three-of-a-kind score, as follows: four 1's = 2,000, four 6's = 1,600, four 5's = 1,500, and so forth.

    And if you throw five of a kind, add 2,000 to your three-of-a-kind score; for six of a kind, add 3,000.

Note that each scoring combination must be achieved in a single throw. For example, if you've set aside two 5's and then you throw a third 5, you don't have a "5" three-of-a-kind.

3. Sounds like a straightforward question of luck? Here's where skill and daring come in.

    At the beginning of your turn, throw all six dice. If your throw doesn't score any points, your turn ends. But if your roll does score points, then you must set aside one or more "scoring dice" —e.g., a 1 (worth 100 points), or three 4's (400), or a 1 and a 5 (100+50=150); and so forth. Now you must calculate the risks of continuing with your turn. You can "bank" your points—add them to your point total on the scorepad—and end your turn. Or else you can roll the remaining "throwing dice" and attempt to add points to your total for that turn.

Illustrations by Mister Reusch

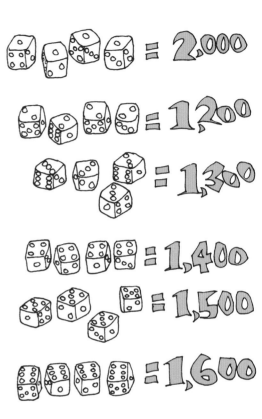

4. Why wouldn't you just keep throwing the dice? Because if you throw the dice and don't score on *any* of them—no 1's, no 5's, no three- or four- or five-of a kinds—then your turn ends *and* you lose all the points you'd accumulated so far during that turn! Failing to score any points on a throw is known, in most variants of the game, as "farkling."

5. However! If you end up scoring on all six dice, then you have what's known as "hot dice." You may now throw all six dice again, and continue adding to your score from that turn. There is no limit to the number of "hot dice" throws a player may roll in one turn. Just don't farkle, or you'll lose that turn's points.

6. Once a player has reached 10,000+ points, he is temporarily the winner. However, each remaining player gets one last chance to surpass the winning player's score.

- Three pair—rolled on a single throw—is worth 500 points.

- A straight (1–2–3–4–5–6) rolled on a single throw is worth 1,000 points.

- Before she can officially join the game, on her turn a player must continue throwing the dice until she banks a minimum of 500 points. If she farkles instead, then she loses her turn.

CUSTOM
DICE GAMES

The following fun games require the purchase of a unique set of dice made specifically for each game.

Pass the Pigs uses two tiny pigs as dice. Scoring the game depends not only on how each pig lands—e.g., on its side, its back, standing up, leaning on its snout—but also on whether and how (e.g., both standing up, both on their sides, snouts together) the pigs are touching.

Cosmic Wimpout is a game from the 1970s that has acquired a cult following, complete with annual tournaments. In addition to numbers, the game's dice feature far-out swirls, triangles, lightning bolts, stars, and a flaming sun. PS: The game used to come with Cosmic Wimpout stickers that—once upon a time—you'd spot almost everywhere you traveled.

Cthulhu Dice gets its name from the creepy science-fiction stories of H.P. Lovecraft, which feature a tentacled creature so awesomely horrible that the mere sight of it can cause madness. The symbols on the game's 12-sided die include a tentacle, an eye, and Cthulhu! The objective of the game is to be the last sane player left.

Zombie Dice is a game from the zombies' point of view. The game's 6-sided dice feature symbols representing runners (potential victims), shotgun blasts (potential victims, fighting back), and—of course—brains (yum). The object is to be the first zombie to eat 13 brains.

JUMP ROPE!

If you get bored with normal rope skipping, try these variations. For each of these games, you'll need a long jump rope.

Complete 10 jumps without spilling the water!

WATER SPLASH
Players: 3+

You'll need:
• A cup of water for each player

Try this:
1. Each player takes a turn jumping while holding a cup of water, completing at least 10 consecutive jumps. Try not to spill! The players turning the rope must keep it nice and steady.

2. When each player has completed 10 jumps without spilling water, do a new round with 15 jumps. Increase by five jumps each round. When one only player has water left, he's the winner.

HELICOPTER
Players: 4+

Try this:
1. One person (the spinner) holds one handle of the jump rope. The other players form a circle around the spinner.

2. The spinner twirls rapidly around, holding the jump rope low to the ground. Pretend it's a helicopter propeller—the other players must leap up to avoid it. If they're hit, they're eliminated. Whoever is the last player to survive the helicopter propellor becomes the spinner.

Illustrations by Heather Kasunick

SNAKE IN THE GRASS

Players: 3+

Try this:

1. Two rope turners kneel on the ground and move the rope from side to side, so that it slithers like a snake. The rope can move fast, slow, or a combination of both.

2. On your turn, try to jump over the "snake" without landing on it. If you touch the rope, you're eliminated. Whoever is the last player to survive the snake wins the game.

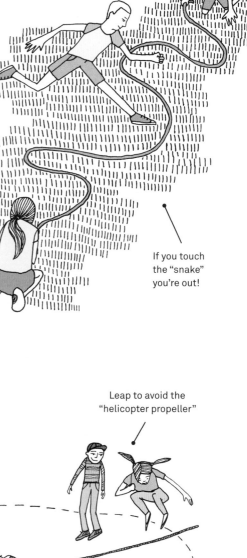

If you touch the "snake" you're out!

➡ HACKS

- **Build a house** Two players hold the rope a few inches off the floor. Each player jumps over the "house" and back. Once everyone has had a turn, the rope holders raise it a little.

- **Ocean waves** Two players kneel on the ground and move the rope up and down quickly. Each player jumps over the "waves" and back.

Leap to avoid the "helicopter propeller"

The spinner twirls the jump rope low to the ground

6th century BC

The Greeks invent spheristics, where the player who tosses an object farthest wins. The game evolves into boules, which is French for "round heavy ball." Also called Bocce, it's still popular and is played in town squares or parks.

5th century BC

The Chinese go nuts for Jianzi, where players keep a shuttlecock from touching the ground by using any part of their body except their hands. By 1972, a modification of jianzi is invented in Oregon. Its name? Hacky Sack.

27 BC–393 AD

Kids in the Early Roman Empire mimic soldiers-in-training by leaping around on courts 100 feet in length. This game eventually turns into hopscotch.

THE SECRET HISTORY

1600s

Modern-day lacrosse is invented when Native American communities create games where a ball—sometimes made of deer hair and hide—is tossed into the air and hit with sticks.

1800s

Stickball, a pick-up game of baseball that uses a broom handle and rubber ball, is a hit across the northeastern United States. Rules are modified to fit the situation. A manhole cover, for example, can be used as a base.

c.1917

Originally called "Kick Baseball," kickball is invented by Nicholas C. Seuss, Supervisor of Cincinnati Park Playgrounds in Ohio. Gym teachers then use the game to teach boys and girls the basics of baseball.

a 2nd century AD

Legend has it that workers who set up camp for the Greek armies pick up discarded horseshoes and create a game by throwing them at a stake in the ground.

7th century AD

Skilled Chinese rope makers create a game called Hundred Rope Jumping, which becomes a favorite sport of Chinese New Year festivals.

1500s

Kids and adults in Tudor-era England play blind man's bluff. The person who is "it" wears a blindfold and tries to tag other players.

OF OUTDOOR GAMES

1962

Kick the can becomes so popular that it's featured on the hit TV show THE TWILIGHT ZONE. If you don't know how to play this street game, ask a grownup to show you how. You'll be glad you did.

1964

Chemist Norman Stingley invents the SuperBall, an awesomely bouncy rubber ball that can be used to play jacks and other outdoor games.

1990s

Pogs goes mainstream, spreading from Hawaii—where it was invented in the 1920s—to the rest of the U.S. The game's name comes from POG, a brand of Hawaiian juice. The juice's bottle tops were originally used as the discs.

OH SNAP!
COMPLICATED CLAPPING

The leader calls out a category

cities!

In our previous book, *Unbored*, we described several classic clapping games and rhymes. Here are a few more that are even trickier to master.

CONCENTRATION

Players: 2+, the more the merrier

This game tests your ability to remember stuff—people, places, and things from various categories that are called out—while keeping a steady clapping rhythm going. It's tough!

Try this:

1. Practice the following *slap-clap-snap-snap* rhythm until everyone has got it down:

   • Slap your knees with both hands.
   • Clap your hands together.
   • Snap your fingers, first one hand and then the other.

Boston!

Each person calls out an example from the category

2. Assign someone the job of being the game leader. After several rounds of the *slap-clap-snap-snap* sequence, the leader says—each syllable of this phrase matching one of the beats of the rhythm—"Con-cen-tra-tion is the ga-ame/ Keep the rhy-thm all the sa-ame." (If this is done correctly, your snaps will coordinate with "ga-ame" and "sa-ame.")

3. The leader then calls out a category: "Vegetables," for example, or "Cities," "Teachers," "Sports," "Movie stars," and so forth. Moving around the circle clockwise from the game's leader, each person calls out a person, place, or thing from that category: "Carrot," for example, or "Chicago," "Mrs. Hernandez," "Volleyball," "Brad Pitt."

4. Continue around the circle until a player can't think of an example, or until someone breaks the rhythm. Assign a new leader, and start over.

3. Clap your hands together once and say—you guessed it—"Clap."

4. With your right fist, hit your breastbone twice and say, "Ba-boom."

5. Snap the fingers on your right hand and say, "Snap."

6. Clap your hands together and say, "Clap."

7. Snap the fingers on your right hand and say, "Snap."

BOOM, SNAP, CLAP

Players: 1 or 2

No quick thinking required for this game. Just lots of practice and coordination.

Try this:

1. With the open palm of your right hand, slap your breastbone once and say, "Boom."

2. Snap the fingers on your right hand once and say, "Snap."

8. With the open palm of your right hand, slap your breastbone once and say, "Boom."

Illustrations by Mister Reusch

9. Snap the fingers on your right hand once and say, "Snap."

10. Clap your hands together once and say "Clap."

11. With your right fist, hit your breastbone twice and say, "Ba-boom."

12. Snap the fingers on your right hand and say, "Snap."

13. Put your right finger to your mouth and say, "Shhh."

14. Do it all again, faster. "Boom, snap, clap. Ba-boom, snap, clap, snap. Boom, snap, clap. Ba-boom, snap, shh!"

15. Repeat.

➡ HACKS

- Instead of clapping, slap your knees, feet, or elbows. (But say "Clap.")
- Each new round, replace "shhh" with a different word and hand gesture.
- Play with a friend! On the "clap" beat, instead of clapping your own hands together, clap each other's hands.

BO-BO-SKI-WATTEN-TATTEN

Players: 2+, the more the merrier

If you search YouTube for this folk clapping game (it's spelled lots of different ways), you'll find a plethora of clapping-slapping-snapping variations. We'll let you invent your own! Each time you repeat the rhymes and clapping, hide a different body part.

Bo-bo-ski-watten-tatten,
Ah-ah, ah-ah, boom-boom-boom
Itty-bitty-watten-tatten
Bo-bo-ski-watten-tatten
Bo-bo-ski-watten-tatten
Freeze, please, American cheese

Stop clapping. Pull your lips over your teeth.

Please don't show your teeth to me!

Bo-bo-ski-watten-tatten,
Ah-ah, ah-ah, boom-boom-boom
Itty-bitty-watten-tatten
Bo-bo-ski-watten-tatten
Bo-bo-ski-watten-tatten
Freeze, please, American cheese

Stop clapping. Close your eyes.

Please don't show your eyes to me!

DANCE-OFF

A dance-off is a competitive game where two people, or two teams, take turns trying to outdo each other with increasingly difficult dance moves.

The way grownups dance can be seriously embarrassing, we know. So here are a few tips for making your family's informal dance-offs fun, while helping grownups retain their self-esteem.

Get inspired

Search YouTube for "dance-off" to give your grownup the basic idea of the game's rules. Decide, for example, whether competitors will dance one at a time or in groups. You can also practice for your family's dance-off by playing videogames like *Dance Dance Revolution*, *Just Dance*, or *Dance Central*.

Agree on a playlist

You might love dubstep, but your dance-off will stink if your grownup doesn't know how to dance to it. Before you begin, choose 5–10 songs that everybody likes.

Set the mood

You can have a dance-off in your living room or kitchen—anywhere with enough space to bust some moves. Move furniture out of the way, and dim the lights.

Start easy

For the first rounds, keep your dancing on the simple side. Start with some chest pops or easy robot moves (your grownup might surprise you by how good she is at these). Save the windmills, headspins, and jackhammers for later rounds.

Go freestyle

The most important thing about a dance-off is having fun. If your grownup prefers disco, air guitar, or Irish step-dancing, do not make fun of him! Even though dance-offs are competitive, it's important to always cheer for your opponent.

Don't twerk

Or grind, or attempt any of the other inappropriate moves that might be popular at your school dances. Your grownup's heart will already be racing—you don't want to kill him.

Illustrations by Mister Reusch

SECRET-RULES
GAMES

A secret-rules game is one in which the game's rules are concealed from new players... because figuring out the rules is an important part of the game itself.

My new rule: anyone who plays a 5 skips a turn.

This game of Mau has officially begun.

These games reward players who are good at inductive reasoning, i.e., the scientific method of observation, hypothesis forming, and trial-and-error experimentation. Making mistakes is part of the fun!

MAU
Players: 3+

This addictive card game is similar to *Uno* or Crazy Eights—i.e., a player may play any card in her hand that matches either the value (e.g., Ace, King, Queen, etc.) or the suit (Spades, Hearts, Diamonds, Clubs) of the face-up card. The object is to be the first player to get rid of all your cards. That's the only thing a new player is told about the rules of Mau.

You'll need:
- A deck of playing cards. Are you a few cards short of a full deck? Doesn't matter!
- At least one player who knows the rules of Mau.

Try this:

1. The dealer deals the same number of cards to each player—usually between three and seven. The remaining cards are placed face-down in a stack. The top card from the stack is turned over and placed next to it. The dealer says, "This game of Mau has officially begun."

2. The player to the left of the dealer goes first; the play continues clockwise. If a player cannot play, then she must draw a new card and place it into her hand—and the turn passes to the next player. When one player succeeds in getting rid of all her cards, the game ends.

3. Sounds simple, right? Not so fast! There are all sorts of rules to Mau, governing everything from which card causes the order of play to reverse (e.g., from clockwise to counter-clockwise),

Illustrations by Heather Kasunick

to which cards are wild, to which card must be named aloud when played, to which card forces the next player to draw a penalty card *and* forces the player who played it to utter a particular phrase (e.g., "Have a nice day"). There is a rule governing what any player who has only one card remaining, or who plays her final card, must say. *But we're not allowed to tell you those rules.* So find someone who knows the rules, or make up your own.

4. A player who breaks any of these rules is penalized by being given an additional card from the stack; the player giving the penalty—any player can do so—must state what the incorrect action was, without explaining the rule that was broken. For example, let's imagine that one of the rules is: "If a player plays an Ace, then the next player skips a turn." If an Ace is played, and the next player goes ahead and puts down a card (whoops!), then someone should hand the offender a penalty card from the deck and announce, simply, "Penalty for playing out of order." New players who observe this penalty might suspect that if a player plays an Ace, then the following player skips a turn—so next time an Ace is played, they'll see if their guess is right.

5. Sound complicated? It gets trickier! The winner of each round of Mau not only deals the next round, they invent a new rule for that round—*which, of course, they won't announce.*

SCISSORS
Players: 4+

This parlor game dates back to the 19th century. Although its rules may seem incredibly complex—baffling, even—to a new player, a little sharp observation will reveal the not-so-complex truth.

You'll need:
- A pair of scissors.
- At least two players who know the rules of Scissors.

Try this:

1. Stand in a circle. The game won't work sitting around a table.

2. The first player hands the scissors— they should be closed—to the person on his right. (Note that these two players must know the game's rules!) The second player, who was standing with his legs apart, says, "I received these scissors uncrossed and I give them crossed." He opens the scissors and

APP FUN WITH
MARK & JANE!

Q&A with Mark & Jane Frauenfelder

There are over a million apps out there. So how do kids and their grownups decide which ones to try?

Since 2011, the podcast *Apps for Kids* (boingboing.net/tags/appsforkids) has reviewed one app per week. The podcast is co-hosted by 10-year-old Jane Frauenfelder and her father Mark, who is editor-in-chief of the magazine *MAKE*.

UNBORED: Jane, what do you and your mom and dad prefer to play—boardgames or apps?

JANE: There are some toys, like LEGO, that are more fun than any app. But I like apps better than most boardgames, because they're more complex—more stuff happens in them, there are more surprises. You have to make more decisions, and make them quicker. And they're easier to take with you when you're on car trip or waiting at a restaurant.

MARK: I agree, and also—speaking as a grownup—I appreciate how tidy apps are. When our family plays the boardgame *Carcassonne*, the pieces end up all over

the place, but when we play the app version of the game we're just passing the iPad back and forth. Also, the app is easier to play—it lets you know which moves are legal or illegal, you don't have to look it up in the rulebook. However, I should mention that one boardgame we love is Chinese Checkers.

JANE: Yeah, Chinese Checkers is way more fun as a boardgame than as an app. And unlike most boardgames for kids, you don't just follow instructions when you play Chinese Checkers—you have to really strategize. So if you win the game, it's a real accomplishment.

Photo courtesy Mark Frauenfelder

Many grownups worry that apps are just a mindless way to waste time.

MARK: I do like it when Jane puts away the iPad and draws something in her invention notebook. If she was on screens all the time, we'd be very concerned. Her mother is more concerned about it than I am. But we're not nearly as worried as some parents, who just think apps and videogames are nothing but bleeps and bloops and shapes moving on a screen.

UNBORED: **Where and when do you most often play apps?**

JANE: I'm allowed to play apps for one hour a day during the week, and two hours a day on weekends. So during the week I mostly play apps after I'm done with dinner and my homework. Or if I want a break from my homework, I might play a little bit after school.

MARK: We also play at restaurants, when we're waiting to be served. Recently, when we were at a Japanese restaurant, we started playing an origami-folding app that was so fun we were almost disappointed when the food arrived.

JANE: When we're on trips, or waiting in a long line, we also like *Story Dice*. The app rolls virtual dice with symbols on them—a ghost, a bicycle, a snowflake—and you compete to make up the best story based on those symbols. If I was a kid whose parents didn't like apps, I'd tell them a great story I'd made up by playing *Story Dice*. When they asked me, "Where'd you hear that?" I'd say, "An app encouraged me to use my imagination. That's where!"

THERE'S AN
APP FOR THAT

Mark and Jane have played and reviewed dozens of fun smartphone apps for kids and parents. Here are their favorites so far.

Sword of Fargoal
All the fun of a classic dungeoncrawler like *Rogue*, but with a spooky soundtrack and appealing graphics.

Kingdom Rush
The best tower defense game. Manage your resources to fight off an invading horde.

Plants vs. Zombies 2
Requires a chess-like strategy when setting your zombie-smashing plants in the right place on your lawn.

Robot Wants Kitty
Your robot must acquire special skills to navigate through a hazardous environment to recover a lost kitty.

Jetpack Joyride
How long can you avoid or destroy obstacles as you fly with your high-speed jetpack?

Windosill
Absurd, gorgeous, surreal puzzle game.

Flow Free
Connect matching colors by dragging pipes from one dot to another. It gets difficult fast!

Subway Surfers
You take on the role of a graffiti artist in a train yard and must escape a security guard and his fierce dog—while dodging speeding trains.

Video Star
This easy-to-use app lets you make cool special-effects videos of your favorite songs.

Dungeon Raid
Like *Candy Crush*, but with monsters.

GAME NIGHT!

By Catherine Newman

Light a fire

Gather up blankets and pillows

Why do you want to bug your grownups to have a regular family game night?

"Um, because it's *awesome*?" (That's what my daughter Birdy, who is ten, said when I asked. My 14-year-old son, Ben, agreed.)

That's the main reason. But I've also heard that playing games with your family is important because games are pointless. In a good way. A game is pure leisure—something you do just to spend time together having fun. When you play a game with your family, you are saying to each other, "I want to be with you." Which is a nice thing to say.

Want to make every game night the best night ever? Try the following tips.

Really make the time

This means everyone comes to the game relaxed and undistracted. If your grownups need help remembering to leave their phones and devices turned off, please remind them.

Pick the right game

My family uses different methods to pick games. Sometimes we'll be in a such an intense phase of playing a particular game that the choice is obvious (e.g., *Agricola*, for all of 2012). Other times someone will have a hankering that the rest of us are willing to accommodate: "Ooooh, would everyone be happy to play Chinese Checkers?"

GAME-NIGHT
FAVORITES
By Catherine Newman

Acquire
You're trying to control the biggest hotel chains on the board; it's like *Monopoly* on steroids.

Agricola
Two hours of your life will whiz by in a blur of delightful farm-themed anxiety while you try to feed your people and expand your house and do a million more things that you *don't have enough time to do.*

Big Boggle
Like the game you know, only bigger.

Chinese Checkers
Another game you know, but Google "Super Jumping" and use it.

Dominion
You're trying to amass resources, and do things in the right order in a crazy algorithm of logic and strategy. And if you need more, there are a million expansions.

Dutch Blitz
With a simple Solitaire-style of play (stacking consecutive cards) this one's all about speed and concentration. Plus, it's short and good with two, three, or four people.

Love Letter
Easy to learn, relatively quick, and like a cross between Hearts, *Stratego*, and a Jane Austen novel. Plus, it comes in a velvet draw-string bag.

Make Me a Cake
We play this when Birdy craves a "non-thinking" game. The pieces are pretty and sparkly, and the cakes are glam and gorgeous. Who won? Who cares.

Settlers and Seafarers of Catan
Classic strategy games where you gather resources to build settlements, cities, and roads.

Stone Age
This is another one of those not-enough-turns-to-do-everything strategy games. You need more people to get more stuff, but the more people you have, the more food you must gather to feed them. Aaaagh!

Sometimes we pick a game based on how much time we have, or what kind of mood everyone's in (if some of us have been bickering, then it's better not to pick a really crazy-competitive game like *Acquire*). If it's a weekend day or a vacation night, we sometimes do "everyone picks a game" and play them all in a row—usually a mix of epic strategy games like *The Seafarers of Catan* and shorter games like *Dutch Blitz* or *Love Letter*.

We've even turned picking games into a game. We create a list of all the games we want to play, then we each put a number next to each game on the list—from 4 (the one we most want to play) to 1 (the one we least want to play). We play the game with the highest total score.

Don't get stuck in a rut

If you don't have enough games that people are excited to play, borrow or trade games with another family—and get them to teach it to you first, since it's much easier to learn from players than from written rules. Or see if your local game store has a time when you can try out different games.

Get comfy

Light a fire in your woodstove if it's chilly; turn music on or off; gather up blankets and pillows if you're sitting on the floor; and make good snacks. In the winter we make a pot of vanilla-scented tea. In the summer we'll put out icy glasses of seltzer and a bowl of grapes. At all times of year, even though greasy fingers and games don't mix, we'll pop some popcorn.

Play well together

You already know that *Big Boggle* is good for your vocabulary, and strategy games give your brain a workout. But games let you practice social skills and basic courtesy, too: how to cooperate (*Pandemic*); how to deal with being jerked around (*Sorry!*); how to be patient (you need to pay attention when other people are taking their turn and you need to be mindful, when it's your turn, that other people are waiting); how to handle stress; and—most importantly—how to win or lose graciously.

> **IMPORTANT!** If there are very young people in your family, encourage them to join game night by picking a game they love, even if it's *Candy Land*. You can play more challenging games after they go to bed.

Always win (or lose) graciously

In Wink Murder, it's important for victims to die dramatically

PARLOR GAMES

Players: 4+, the more the merrier

Before the invention of boardgames, not to mention radio, movies, and TV, parlor games were popular in England and the United States. Parlor games involve sophisticated word-play, dramatic skill, cultural knowledge, and sometimes a little bit of good-humored roughhousing.

Illustrations by Heather Kasunick

You may already be familiar with parlor games like Charades, Twenty Questions, and Dictionary; here are a few fun ones that we play with our families.

Wink Murder

In each round of Wink Murder, one player is randomly assigned the role of Murderer, and one the role of Detective; the other players are Victims.

Write "Murderer" and "Detective" on slips of paper, mix them up with other slips that read "Victim," and have everyone pick a slip out of a bowl.

The players sit in a circle; everyone must be able to see everyone else's face. The Detective reveals her identity to the group, then the round begins. One by one, the Murderer makes eye contact with a Victim and "murders" him—by winking at him. (If you are winked at, you must "die" dramatically.) The objective of the Murderer is to wink-murder as many players as possible before the Detective identifies him. The objective of the Detective is to identify and accuse the Murderer. She may only make one accusation; if she guesses incorrectly, the Murderer wins.

Wink Murder variations

There are several variants of Wink Murder. In one, the Detective must sit in the center of the circle of players. In another, the Detective is allowed to make one or two wrong accusations. In another variant, an Accomplice may kill one Victim; if she is accused, the Murderer wins.

In the game Vampire Murder, the Murderer is a Vampire; she kills not by winking but by baring her teeth.

First Sentence

Also known as The Book Game, the only equipment required for First Sentence is pencils, identical slips of paper, and a pile of mass-market paperbacks.

One player picks a book; she is that round's designated Reader. The Reader shows the others the book's cover, reads the description from its back cover, then copies the book's first sentence onto a slip of paper.

Each of the other players takes a few minutes to dream up a possible first sentence for that book: if it's a romance, for example, the first sentence might be something like, "Laura had been watching Harold for days." Each player writes his or her made-up sentence onto a slip of paper, signs his or her initials underneath it, and hands the slip to the Reader.

The Reader reads each slip silently to herself, shuffles all the slips up, then reads them aloud. Each player then votes on which sentence he or she suspects is the real one, from the actual book.

If you correctly deduce the actual first sentence, you are awarded 2 points; if someone votes for your invented sentence, you are awarded 1 point. Keep track of your points—after each player has had a chance to be the Reader, whoever has earned the highest score is the winner.

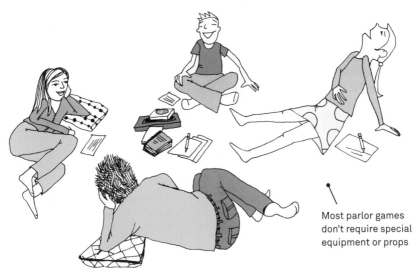

Most parlor games don't require special equipment or props

Coffeepot

One player leaves the room; the others choose an activity that she commonly performs. For example: "ride the bus to school," "watch baseball on TV." The player who left the room is then called back in. She tries to discover what the mystery activity is by asking yes/no questions, substituting the word "coffee-pot" for the verb. For example: "Do I coffeepot outdoors?" "Do I coffeepot with friends?" She continues until she's figured it out; or you can give her a certain number of tries.

A Coffeepot variation

Here's another version of Coffeepot. One player leaves the room; the others choose a common noun or verb.

The first player returns, and tries to discover the mystery word by asking each player a different question. The answers don't need to be truthful, but they must include the mystery word—however, instead of actually saying that word, the player says "coffeepot."

For example, if the mystery word is "minivan," and the first question is, "What does your family do for fun?" the answer might be: "We take our coffeepot to the park and go rollerblading." If the second question is, "Who is your favorite movie monster?" the answer might be: "King Kong, because he squashes coffee-pots as he stomps down the street."

Guess a name that begins with R

Rihanna?

Ryan Seacrest.

Rosa Parks?

Botticelli

Though it began as a parlor game, Botticelli is fun on car trips, too.

The Chooser thinks of a famous person, announces the first letter of their name (last name, usually; but if that makes the game too difficult, it can be either a first or last name), then answers questions asked by the other players (the Guessers). The mystery figure might be a president, athlete, musician, or actor, for example; or perhaps a fictional character from a novel, cartoon show, or comic book.

No fair picking someone obscure! The figure has to be very famous—like Shaquille O'Neal, Scooby-Doo, Taylor Swift, Hermione Granger, or Spider-Man.

A Guesser must think of a famous person or character whose name begins with the same first letter as the mystery figure's name; for example, if the mystery figure is *American Idol* host Ryan Seacrest, and the initial announced is "R," perhaps a Guesser will think of Rosa Parks. Using some detail about Rosa Parks, the Guesser would then ask the Chooser an indirect question; in this case, the question might be: "Are you a civil rights activist?"

If the Chooser replies, "No, I am not Rosa Parks," then it becomes another Guesser's turn.

The Yes/No round

If the Chooser replies, "I give up," because she can't think of anyone who fits the criteria, then the Guesser reveals who they were thinking of, and asks the Chooser direct yes/no questions about the mystery figure—continuing to do so until the Chooser answers with a "No." ("Are you a real person?" "Yes." "Are you a man?" "Yes." "Are you on television?" "Yes." "Are you an actor?" "No.")

How to win (or lose) Botticelli

If a Guesser deduces the mystery figure's identity ("You're Ryan Seacrest!"), then he becomes the next Chooser; however, if the Guesser is mistaken in his guess, then he's out of the game. If every Guesser guesses incorrectly, or if they're all stumped, then the Chooser wins.

HAIR DRYER
PING PONG

Guide the ping pong ball into the bucket

Players: 2+

A scientific principle known as the Bernoulli Effect explains why an airplane's wings make it possible for a heavy plane to lift off the ground. Thanks to the same principle, you can play the following game.

You'll need:
- A standard-size hair dryer (not travel size)
- Several ping pong balls
- A bucket
- An extension cord

1. Stand next to the bucket, with the ping pong balls close at hand. Plug in the hair dryer.

2. Set the hair dryer to its cool setting (to conserve energy), and turn it on. Point it so that the air is shooting toward the ceiling. Place a ping pong ball into the airstream so that it floats.

3. Gently tilt the hair dryer until the ping pong ball falls out of the airstream—the idea is to drop the ball into the bucket. You score 2 points for each ball that remains in the bucket, and 1 point for each ball that bounces out of the bucket. Whoever scores the highest wins.

➡ **HACKS**

- Replace the bucket with a smaller container—try a cereal bowl or even a cup.

- Using the extension cord—so you don't yank the hair dryer's plug out of the socket—move around the room attempting to drop ping pong balls into a variety of buckets, bowls, and cups. It's hair dryer ping pong golf! Assign each "hole" points based on how difficult the challenge is.

Illustrations by Mister Reusch

Whoever finds the trinket wins!

BAKE A GAME

Players: 4+

In New Orleans and elsewhere in the southern U.S., people celebrate Mardi Gras by eating King Cake— a ring-shaped Danish with a trinket (usually a plastic baby, said to represent Baby Jesus) hidden inside. According to the rules of this 17th-century European game, whoever finds the trinket in their slice is awarded the honor of baking the cake for the next celebration.

There are many variations for the recipe, but we like this cream cheese version best.

You'll need:

Dough
- 1 envelope instant yeast
- ½ cup milk
- ¼ cup butter (softened)
- 2 tablespoons sugar
- ¼ teaspoon salt
- 1 egg, room temperature
- 2½ cups flour

Filling
- 10 ounces of cream cheese
- ¼ cup sugar
- 1 teaspoon lemon zest
- 1 teaspoon vanilla

Illustration by Mister Reusch

Icing

- 2 cups powdered sugar
- 2 tablespoons milk
- 1 teaspoon vanilla
- Colored sugar (green, purple, and yellow—if you want to be traditional)

Trinket

You can order King Cake babies online, but feel free to customize your trinket. For example, in some countries an uncooked fava bean is used. A penny wrapped in tinfoil also works.

Try this:

1. Heat milk—don't boil!—in a small saucepan over low heat. Place milk in a bowl, add yeast, and stir to combine. Set aside for 10 minutes or until frothy.

2. Beat the egg in a small bowl and add to milk mixture. Then add the flour, butter, sugar, and salt. Mix on low speed until dough comes together (use a dough hook attachment if you have one). The dough should be slightly sticky. If the dough is too moist, add a tiny bit of flour.

3. Put dough on a lightly floured surface and knead for a few minutes until it's soft. Place in a lightly oiled bowl and cover with a towel or plastic wrap. Allow dough to rise for about an hour, or until it doubles in size. (Keep the bowl in a place that's warm—not next to an open window.)

4. For the filling, beat the cream cheese, vanilla, lemon zest, and sugar together in a clean bowl with a mixer until fluffy.

5. Place dough on lightly floured surface, punch it down and roll it into a 20"x10" rectangle. Spread cream cheese mixture evenly on one half of the long side of the rectangle. Fold the other half over to cover. Pinch dough together to seal in cream cheese. Connect and pinch the ends together to form a ring. Place on a parchment-lined cookie sheet, cover with plastic wrap, and allow to rise for 45 minutes.

6. Pre-heat the oven to 375 degrees. Bake cake for 20 minutes, or until slightly browned. Remove from oven and cool. Make a small slit in the bottom of the ring, and insert the trinket.

7. Mix icing ingredients together and whisk until smooth. Drizzle icing over the cake. Sprinkle with colored sugar while it's still wet.

➡ HACKS

Make a trinket cake for any celebration. A traditional Irish fortune-telling game (played around Halloween) is barmbrack, a fruit bread with charms baked inside. Your future is decided by which charm you get. For example:

- A wedding ring means you'll get married within the year.
- A coin means you'll have good luck or be rich.

Some people even bake coins (covered in tinfoil) into birthday cakes.

EMBRACE SCREENS

Introduce your grownups to games they'll want to play with you

Illustrations by Mister Reusch

Nothing ratchets up a grownup's anxiety more than watching a child stare at a screen. And yet, unless it's almost impossible for you to release your grip on a videogame controller, there's no reason for your grownups to panic.

You can calm grownups down—and possibly increase your screen time—by encouraging them to place restrictions not on the technology itself, but on how and when it's used. Together, sit down and come up with screen time limits for weekdays and weekends. (That is if they can tear themselves away from their *own* screen diversions!) Also, decide together which games are OK to play and which aren't. Then, stick to these ground rules. If your grownups are still squeamish about screens and screen time, get sneaky and invite them to play games with you. Here are a few of our favorites.

Get educational

Grownups love educational activities that are building kids' brains. *Scratch* is an intuitive and fun programming language developed by the MIT Media Lab that you can use—with or without a grownup's help—to create videogames, animations, interactive stories, and art. PS: *Super Scratch Programming Adventure!* is a companion book that teaches you how to build lots of creative (and increasingly complicated) games.

Go easy

If your grownups feel overwhelmed by the thought of programming a game, try introducing them to a mobile or tablet game that's so simple and amusing they'll be charmed into playing it with you again and again. In addition to popular games like *Doodle Jump, Dots, Flow Free, Candy Crush Saga,* and *Angry Birds,* grownups and kids alike enjoy *Scribblenauts, Tug the Table, Samurai Duel,* and *Toca Band.*

Be a copilot

Waze is a social GPS navigation app with a cute interface that allows drivers to earn points by reporting traffic or road hazards, gasoline prices, map problems, and more. On some holidays, *Waze* adds festive icons of "road goodies" to the map; users get points for driving over the goodies. The only problem is that it is *not* safe for a car's driver to use while driving! That's where kids come in—as Chewbaccas to their grownups' Han Solos.

Name that tune

When you and your grownup are listening to the radio, switch on the mobile music identification app *Shazam.* (Other mobile song ID services include *SoundHound* and *musiXmatch.*) Race to identify old songs before your grownup can dredge the same info up from her own age-challenged database.

Navigate traffic and road hazards for your grownup with *Waze*

BEST EVER

APPS TO PLAY WITH A GROWNUP

In what is known as an OTB game of chess, players sit "over the board" together—in the same room, at the same time. Centuries ago, however, chess players discovered that playing long-distance games by sending moves back and forth through the mail can also be a fun way to stay in touch with someone.

An OTB game with a grandparent, parent, or other grownup isn't always possible at the exact moment when you want to play. That's why we recommend the following social apps. They're a great way to say, "Hi! I miss you. Now get ready for me to win."

Draw Something

Omgpop.com/drawsomething
On your turn, choose from one of three guesswords provided by the game, then—using your finger to "draw" on the screen—create a picture which conveys that word. Once you've finished, the game's other player will see your drawing, the guessword's scrambled-up letters, and (for the sake of confusion) a few extra

Spaceteam is a cooperative game that requires players to be in the same room

letters. If she can correctly guess the word that you've illustrated, then you'll *both* win points. The idea is to swap drawings back and forth for as many rounds as possible. Once you've earned enough points, you can trade them in for more shades of color to draw with and other helpful tools.

PS: *Draw Something 2* features thousands of new words, dozens of new drawing tools (including pattern and stamps), and allows you to share your drawings with others.

Illustration by Mister Reusch

LetterPress

Atebits.com/letterpress

This is an addictive combination of a word-hunt game like *Boggle* and a territory-capturing game like *Risk* or *Go*. On your turn, you can use any of the letters on a five-by-five grid of assorted letters to form a word; any of the letters that you use turn blue. Letters used by your opponent to form a word turn pink. Once all of the letters on the grid have been used at least once apiece, the game ends—and if more letters are blue than pink, you win! The territory-capturing aspect makes the game strategic: If you completely surround a blue tile with other blue tiles, then your opponent can't turn it pink, and vice versa.

PS: *LetterPress* is a game for the iPhone or iPad. Grandparents and other grownups will really enjoy playing this game with you, but first you might need to help them navigate Apple's social gaming network Game Center. Which may require some patience on your part.

PaperToss Friends

Backflipstudios.com/games/paper-toss-friends

Score points by tossing a wad of paper—or a stapler, a tomato, a paper airplane, or another object—into a trash can. Sound simple? There's a virtual fan blowing near-by… and it affects the trajectory of lighter objects more than that of heavier objects. You'll have to calculate the angle of your toss carefully. Also, there are different environments for each round so you might be throwing the object a long distance… or at a moving target. Some of the objects burst or explode! If you out-toss your opponent over three rounds, then you win.

Spaceteam

Sleepingbeastgames.com/spaceteam

This is not a long-distance game, exactly—it's a cooperative party game you can play anywhere on up to four mobile phones or tablets, via WiFi or Bluetooth. You're the pilots of a spaceship, each in charge of a unique section of the ship's control panel. Your control panel is crammed with switches, dials, and buttons controlling crazy-sounding yet crucial functions like the ship's Capacitive Omegasphere, Finite Plexus, and Clip-Jawed Monodish. Above the dashboard, the command bar flashes orders requiring you to flip switches, twirl dials, and punch buttons… the twist being that these orders rarely refer to your own dashboard. So you'll need to shout out the command to your teammates, while listening to their commands. Meanwhile, your dashboard is sparking, shaking, and oozing goo. It's stressful and hilarious.

Words With Friends

Wordswithfriends.com

Both players draw seven letters from a pool, at random. On your turn, you'll place a word on the board; the game will add up your points—taking into account the word point listed on the letters, as well as the board's letter and word multipliers. Each new word played must connect to existing ones. Grandparents tend to like this app better than any other, because it's similar to *Scrabble*. In fact, grandparents will probably beat you easily at this game—after all, they've been building their vocabularies a lot longer than you have.

Warning: Some grandparents like to use the app's chat feature to trash-talk!

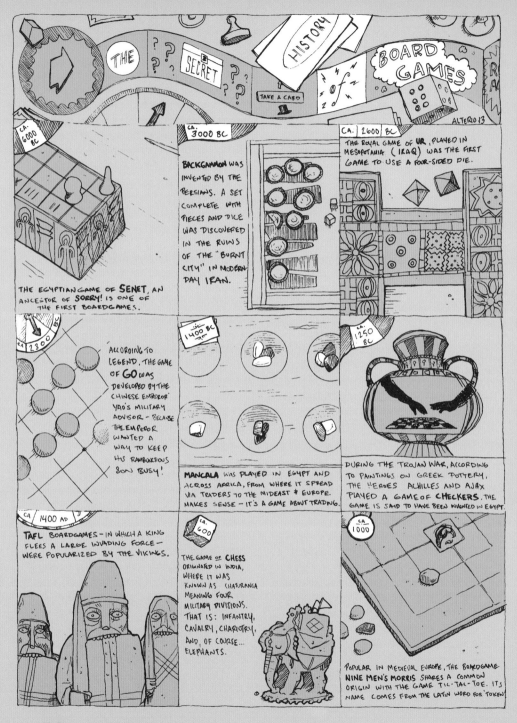

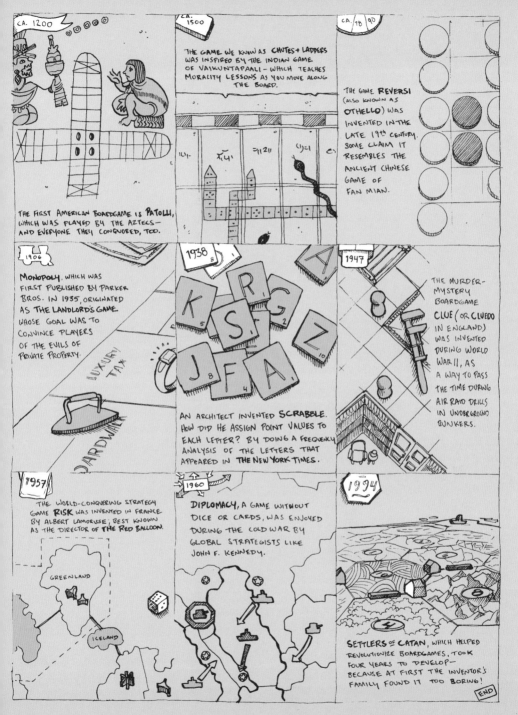

CA. 1200

THE FIRST AMERICAN BOARDGAME IS PATOLLI, WHICH WAS PLAYED BY THE AZTECS— AND EVERYONE THEY CONQUERED, TOO.

CA. 1500

THE GAME WE KNOW AS CHUTES + LADDERS WAS INSPIRED BY THE INDIAN GAME OF VAIKUNTAPAALI — WHICH TEACHES MORALITY LESSONS AS YOU MOVE ALONG THE BOARD.

CA. 1890

THE GAME REVERSI (ALSO KNOWN AS OTHELLO) WAS INVENTED IN THE LATE 19th CENTURY. SOME CLAIM IT RESEMBLES THE ANCIENT CHINESE GAME OF FAN MIAN.

1906

MONOPOLY, WHICH WAS FIRST PUBLISHED BY PARKER BROS. IN 1935, ORIGINATED AS THE LANDLORD'S GAME WHOSE GOAL WAS TO CONVINCE PLAYERS OF THE EVILS OF PRIVATE PROPERTY.

LUXURY TAX

BOARDWALK

1938

AN ARCHITECT INVENTED SCRABBLE. HOW DID HE ASSIGN POINT VALUES TO EACH LETTER? BY DOING A FREQUENCY ANALYSIS OF THE LETTERS THAT APPEARED IN THE NEW YORK TIMES.

1947

THE MURDER-MYSTERY BOARDGAME CLUE (OR CLUEDO IN ENGLAND) WAS INVENTED DURING WORLD WAR II, AS A WAY TO PASS THE TIME DURING AIR RAID DRILLS IN UNDERGROUND BUNKERS.

1957

THE WORLD-CONQUERING STRATEGY GAME RISK WAS INVENTED IN FRANCE BY ALBERT LAMORISSE, BEST KNOWN AS THE DIRECTOR OF THE RED BALLOON.

GREENLAND

ICELAND

1960

DIPLOMACY, A GAME WITHOUT DICE OR CARDS, WAS ENJOYED DURING THE COLD WAR BY GLOBAL STRATEGISTS LIKE JOHN F. KENNEDY.

1994

SETTLERS OF CATAN, WHICH HELPED REVOLUTIONIZE BOARDGAMES, TOOK FOUR YEARS TO DEVELOP— BECAUSE AT FIRST THE INVENTOR'S FAMILY FOUND IT TOO BORING!

END

BEANBAG TOSS

Players: 2 or 4

Cornhole is a game in which you set up two specially made tables—each with a single hole in its tabletop; each propped up at an angle, their top ends 12" off the ground. The tables should stand about 30' apart.

Standing next to your Cornhole table, you toss beanbags at your opponent's table. Bags that drop into the hole in your opponent's table gain you 3 points apiece; bags that land on the board and stay there are worth 1 point apiece. It's a perfect activity for a backyard party!

Building your own unique set of Cornhole tables takes about three hours… here's how.

> **WARNING!** It's always important to use safety goggles when operating any power tool. Grownup supervision is a must.

You'll need:

- Two 2'x4' sheets of ½"-thick plywood
- Four 8'-long 2x4s
- Four 4½"-long ⅜" diameter carriage bolts
- Four ⅜" flat washers
- Four ⅜" wing nuts
- A box of 2½" wood screws
- Drill and assorted bits (must include a screwdriver bit, and a ⅜" bit)
- Saw
- Jigsaw
- Clamps
- Measuring tape
- Hammer
- Compass drawing tool
- Pencil
- Fine sandpaper
- Safety goggles
- A raised work surface (briefly)
- **Optional:** A drill bit smaller than ⅜", for pre-drilling holes

Illustration by Mister Reusch

Cut the wood

1. For the tables' frame sides, measure and cut four 4' sections of 2x4.

2. For the frame ends, cut four 21" sections of 2x4.

3. For the tables' legs, cut four 16" sections of 2x4.

Build the frame & tabletop

Follow these instructions to make the frame and tabletop for one of the two tables, then repeat for the second.

1. Using the 2½" wood screws, screw the 4' sides and 21" ends of the table's frame together. (Pre-drill the holes first with a drill bit slightly smaller in diameter than the screws.) Make sure to keep all the corners and edges flush, so the tabletop will lie flat on the frame (Figure A).

2. Screw the tabletop onto the frame. Drive one screw apiece (through the tabletop) into each of the frame's four corners—while taking care to avoid hitting the frame's screws. Then, at evenly spaced intervals, drive another two screws apiece through the tabletop into the frame's short edges, and another six screws apiece through the tabletop into the frame's long edges. Sink all 20 screws flush with the tabletop, so that you'll have a nice smooth playing surface (Figures B and C).

3. Decide which (short) end of the table will be its top. Measure 9" from the table's top end, and 12" from either side, then mark that spot with your pencil. Using the compass, draw a 6" circle around this center point. Using the jigsaw, cut out a neat 6" hole (Figures D and E).

Make & install the folding legs

Follow these instructions to make and install the folding legs for one of the two tables, then repeat for the second.

1. Take one of the table's two 16" legs, and—at one end—mark its midpoint (approximately 1¾" from each side) with a long vertical line. Next, measure the same distance (1¾") along the leg from the same end, and mark that point with a horizontal line. Place the compass's point where the lines meet, and draw a half circle extending out to the leg's edges (Figure F).

2. Flip the table upside down, and put a piece of scrap wood in either of its two top corners. Set the table leg next to the scrap wood, with the marked side facing out, and clamp the two pieces of wood to the frame. Place the drill bit on the table leg at the point where the two straight lines meet and drill a ⅜" hole through both the leg and the frame's side (Figure G).

3. Clamp the leg down to your work surface and—using the jigsaw—make rough cuts to its rounded end, following the curved lines you drew using the compass. Don't worry, the leg's rounded end doesn't have to be perfectly round or smooth (Figure H).

D

E

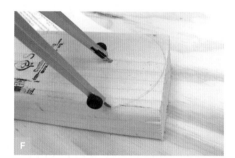

F

G

4. Insert the carriage bolt through the ⅜" hole in the frame's side, and through the ⅜" hole in the leg whose end you've just rounded. Clamp the leg down. Using the hammer, tap the bolt's square "shoulder" into the frame's side until the bolt's head is flush (Figure I). Check to see if the leg can be folded back and forth; if not, do some more rounding work on the leg. Once the leg can be easily folded, put the washer and nut onto the carriage bolt and tighten slightly.

5. Repeat steps 1–4 for the table's second leg. Now you're almost done—except the table's legs are too long, and their "feet" ends won't rest flat on the ground. Mark an "A" on one of the legs and the inside frame edge next to it, and a "B" on the other leg and inside frame edge next to it (Figure J).

6. Next, flip the table right-side up and prop it up on your raised work surface with its legs (fully extended) extending over the work surface's edge. Important! At both corners, the top edge of the table should be exactly 12" off the work table's surface. Measure carefully (Figure K).

7. On each table leg, mark a horizontal line exactly where the leg extends off the edge of your work surface (Figure L). Unbolt the legs from the table, and—using the saw—cut along the lines you've just drawn. It should be approximately a 45-degree cut. Reinstall the table legs (aren't you glad you made the "A" and "B" marks now?) and tighten the nuts on the carriage bolts.

Finishing touches

Sand the tabletop and its edges, as well as the edges and inside of the tabletop's hole. Now build the second table for your Cornhole set. You're ready to play!

Want to paint your Cornhole set? Doing so will preserve the game—and it will look awesome. You might want to use wood putty to fill in the screwholes (we didn't). Then use a quart of primer paint (for wood), plus a quart of semi-gloss latex paint in whatever color you like. (Figure M)

We're very grateful to Matt Glenn and Megan Folz for the construction help.

Once you've built your Cornhole set, you can paint it—or just start playing the game.

NO-SEW BEANBAGS

Inspired by the No-Sew Stuffed Animal in our book *Unbored*, these beanbags won't pass muster with strict Cornhole players... but you can make them quickly and easily.

You'll need:

- 4 socks of one pattern or color, plus 4 socks of another pattern or color
- 64 oz. of unpopped popcorn (because it's Cornhole). Or you could use dried beans.
- 8 resealable sandwich bags
- Duct tape

Try this:

1. Fill the 8 sandwich bags with equal amounts of popcorn or beans.

2. Seal the bags, then cover the seals with duct tape for extra security.

3. Push one filled bag into the toe of each sock, then knot the sock.

TWENTY QUESTIONS

AN EXCERPT FROM

— PETER PAN AND WENDY —

by J.M. Barrie

In a memorable scene from J.M. Barrie's 1911 novel *Peter Pan and Wendy*, Peter Pan, who is pretending to be a spirit, and his piratical enemy Captain Hook play the parlor game Twenty Questions, which first became popular around that time.

Hook raised his voice, but there was a quiver in it.

"Spirit that haunts this dark lagoon to-night," he cried, "dost hear me?"

Of course Peter should have kept quiet, but of course he did not. He immediately answered in Hook's voice:

"Odds, bobs, hammer and tongs, I hear you."

In that supreme moment Hook did not blanch, even at the gills, but Smee and Starkey clung to each other in terror.

"Who are you, stranger? Speak!" Hook demanded.

"I am James Hook," replied the voice, "captain of the *Jolly Roger*."

"You are not; you are not," Hook cried hoarsely.

"Brimstone and gall," the voice retorted, "say that again, and I'll cast anchor in you."

Hook tried a more ingratiating manner. "If you are Hook," he said almost humbly, "come tell me, who am I?"

"A codfish," replied the voice, "only a codfish."

"A codfish!" Hook echoed blankly, and it was then, but not till then, that his proud spirit broke. He saw his men draw back from him.

"Have we been captained all this time by a codfish!" they muttered. "It is lowering to our pride."

They were his dogs snapping at him, but, tragic figure though he had become, he scarcely heeded them. Against such fearful evidence it was not their belief in him that he needed, it was his own. He felt his ego slipping from him. "Don't desert me, bully," he whispered hoarsely to it.

In his dark nature there was a touch of the feminine, as in all the great pirates, and it sometimes gave him intuitions. Suddenly he tried the guessing game.

"Hook," he called, "have you another voice?"

Now Peter could never resist a game, and he answered blithely in his own voice, "I have."

"And another name?"

"Ay, ay."

"Vegetable?" asked Hook.

"No."

"Mineral?"

"No."

"Animal?"

"Yes."

"Man?"

"No!" This answer rang out scornfully.

"Boy?"

"Yes."

"Ordinary boy?"

"No!"

"Wonderful boy?"

To Wendy's pain the answer that rang out this time was "Yes."

"Are you in England?"

"No."

"Are you here?"

"Yes."

Hook was completely puzzled. "You ask him some questions," he said to the others, wiping his damp brow.

Smee reflected. "I can't think of a thing," he said regretfully.

"Can't guess, can't guess!" crowed Peter. "Do you give it up?"

Of course in his pride he was carrying the game too far, and the miscreants saw their chance.

"Yes, yes," they answered eagerly.

"Well, then," he cried, "I am Peter Pan."

CROQUET GOLF

Players: 2+, the more the merrier

Croquet, a genteel English lawn game in which a mallet is used to knock wooden balls through metal "wickets," became a North American fad in the 1890s. One reason the game remains so fun today is because you can hack it to suit the precise shape of your own yard.

Do you have access to a large outdoor space? Then you will enjoy this croquet variant.

You'll need:

- Between 6 and 18 wickets. If you don't have enough, make some out of wire coat hangers.
- Croquet balls, one per player
- Croquet mallets, one per player
- Paper and pencil, for mapping and keeping score.

Try this:

1. Stroll around your playing field and sketch out a course. Decide where the game should begin, where it should end, and how many "holes" (in golf terminology, the area from a teeing ground, down a fairway, and to a putting green) your course will have. For each hole, decide where the teeing ground, fairway, and putting green will be; and place a wicket on the putting green. Finally, assign a number to each hole, in the order that you want them to be played.

Illustrations by Heather Kasunick

2. Take a practice run through the course—the more practice players, the better. For each hole, keep track of how many strokes, on average, are required to get the ball from green to wicket. The number of strokes is known as a hole's "par"; on your map, mark each hole's par.

3. You're ready to play! For each hole, take turns driving your ball from the teeing ground; after that round, whoever's ball is farthest from the wicket gets to go. Once you've each knocked your ball through the wicket, record how many strokes it took each of you to do so. As in golf, you're competing to finish each hole using the fewest possible number of strokes.

⇒ H A C K S

- You can rule that—as in the game of croquet—if you hit another player's ball (doing so is known as "making a roquet"), you get a free shot (known as a "croquet stroke").
- You can add a penalty stroke to a player's score for infraction of croquet rules—e.g., "double tap" or "push." (See sidebar.)

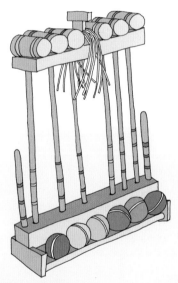

KNOW YOUR
CROQUET LINGO

Ball-in-hand
A ball that a player is allowed to pick up, in order to change its position. For example, a ball that has left the playing field; or a roqueted ball.

Croquet stroke
A free stroke taken after making a roquet.

Double tap
If the mallet makes more than one audible sound when it strikes the ball, then the striker is penalized one stroke.

Push
If the striker's mallet pushes the ball, rather than making a clean strike, then the striker is penalized one stroke.

Roquet
When the striker's ball hits another player's ball.

Striker
The player whose turn it is.

DRAW!

EXQUISITE CORPSE

Players: 3+

This game (also known as Picture Consequences) was invented in the 1920s by the Surrealists—artists and writers who combined realistic imagery with random material from their dreams. Each player draws a separate part of a body (animal, human, whatever) without seeing the other players' drawings until the very end.

You'll need:

- A sheet of paper (printer paper works best), folded vertically in three equal parts
- Pencils

Try this:

1. Not showing anyone else, in the top third of the piece of paper the first player draws the figure's head. On the second section, he marks lines for where the neck ends—so the second player knows where she should start drawing the figure's shoulders. He then folds that section of the paper so that no one can see what has been created, and passes the paper.

2. On the second section of the paper, the second player draws the figure's torso; then she marks lines, on the third section, where the figure's hips should begin. She then folds that section of the paper so that no one can see what has been created, and passes the paper.

3. On the third section of the paper, the third player draws the figure's hips, legs, and feet. Unfold the paper to see what you've created together!

PS: To play with more than three people, fold the paper into smaller sections and assign each player a smaller part of the body, e.g. just the feet or just the top half of the face.

Illustrations by Heather Kasunick

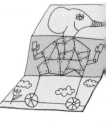

In this game, each player unwittingly changes the story

Grandma moonwalked on Saturn.

Senior citizens will take over the universe

TELEPHONE PICTIONARY

Players: The more the merrier

This game combines aspects of the game Telephone, in which a phrase is whispered from player to player until it changes beyond recognition, and the game *Pictionary*, in which one player draws an object or phrase and the other players try to guess what the drawing is.

You'll need:

- A small pad of paper
- A pencil to share
- Something else to do, while each player takes her turn. The game can take a while!

Try this:

1. On the pad's first sheet of paper, one player writes a phrase—the more absurd the better. (For example: "Grandma moonwalked on Saturn.") The pad is passed to a second player.

2. On the pad's second sheet of paper, the second player draws a picture illustrating the phrase on the first sheet. She then flips the first sheet of paper around... so the third player can only see the second sheet. The pad is passed to a third player.

3. On the pad's third sheet of paper, the third player writes a phrase describing the drawing on the second sheet. She then flips the second sheet of paper around... so the fourth player can only see the third sheet. The pad is passed to a fourth player.

4. Continue, until each player has contributed once to the game. At the end, the first player reads all the phrases aloud—and shows off all the illustrations—to the group, in order.

➡ HACKS

If you have several pads of paper (and pencils) you can get multiple games going more or less at the same time. Just make sure that each player contributes to each game only once; it might be wisest to do this version while sitting in a circle, passing the pads clockwise.

INVENT A GAME!

Q&A with Andrew Innes

Andrew Innes first got the idea for his popular party game, *Anomia*, when he was 12.

The game is deceptively simple: On your turn, you flip over a card from your own draw pile, revealing that card's symbol and its category ("Vegetable," say, or "Comic Book Character"). If the card's symbol matches the symbol on another player's face-up card, then you compete to be the first to finish calling out a word ("Carrot!", "Batman!") that fits the category on each other's card. It's tricky to come up with the right word when you're under pressure.

Working out of his home, Innes sold several hundred copies of *Anomia*, mostly to friends. His game started winning awards—and since then, he's sold over 100,000 copies. He and his wife started a business, and in 2012 they published their second game, *Duple*, which is also a blast. In 2013, they released *Anomia: Party Edition*, which adds six new decks. We asked Innes for some pointers on inventing and developing your own game.

UNBORED: When you're inventing a game, does the idea need to be a brand-new one?

INNES: No. I first got the idea for *Anomia* when I was 12, from Store. Each player would declare what kind of store he had, perhaps a pet shop or a grocery store, then you'd flip over ordinary playing cards.

Illustration by Mister Reusch   Photo courtesy Andrew Innes

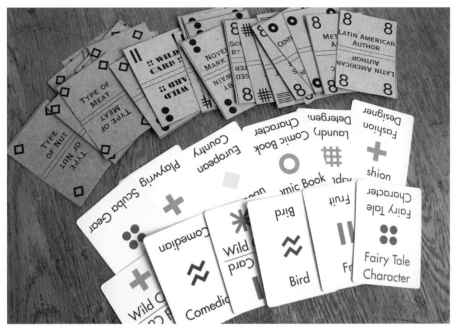

Spot the changes that Andrew made to the prototype of *Anomia*. Both the prototype and the final edition of the game are shown here.

If your card's rank matched the rank of another player's card, you'd both race to yell out something from each other's store: "Dog!" "Milk!" I loved Store because it was intense, like my other favorite game, Spit. Plus, you had to think up all these examples on the fly. But limiting the game's categories to "store" struck me as way too limited.

UNBORED: What's your advice to someone who wants to invent a game?

INNES: Make a prototype and test it. Take feedback from friends, family, and especially strangers, and refine the game multiple times—I played *Anomia* with over 200 people over the course of a few years, before I was ready to take it to market. Make the game as simple as you can, without losing sight of your original idea. Make a game that *you* love to play.

UNBORED: How did the game's mechanics change, thanks to the play-testing that you did?

INNES: My original design was ugly—brown marbled cardstock, black-and-white symbols that were in the card's corner instead of centered. There might have been a dozen symbols on the cards originally, but I whittled them down to eight—because the fewer symbols, the more face-offs. And I added wild cards, because that keeps everyone on their toes.

UNBORED: Did your play-testers also help you test the game's directions?

INNES: You want to make sure that people can learn the game using only the written directions. I used my play-testing events to test the directions, then I spent 60 hours rewriting. I suggest that game inventors get someone to help you edit and copy-edit the directions.

UNBORED: The game's name is Greek for "the inability to recall a word," which makes sense. But the word also means "chaos," and we've noticed that *Anomia* does tend to get chaotic...

Anomia packages: prototype and final.

INNES: Two people race to yell a word that fits into a category. Two categories that have nothing to do with each other are juxtaposed. You're under pressure! So you're jumping up, waving your arms, and making nonsense sounds. It's as much fun to watch as it is to play.

MINDGAME

The Only...
MLB TEAMS

There are currently 30 teams that make up the Major League Baseball (MLB) franchise, 15 in the National League and 15 in the American League. You could write a riveting book about how all the team names originated and how they have evolved over the years. (Did you know there used to be a team called the St. Louis Brown Stockings?) But a book within a book would be a bit weird, so here's a short word puzzle about MLB names instead. Call to mind as many of the 30 current teams you can and remove the geography part. (So if there happened to be an MLB team called the Tallahassee Toilets, you would drop the "Tallahassee" and consider only the "Toilets.")

Then subject your list of abbreviated names to rigorous analysis and answer the following questions:

1. What is the only MLB team that contains exactly five letters?
2. What is the only MLB team that contains more vowels than consonants?
3. What is the only MLB team that begins with the letter N?
4. What is the only MLB team that contains the letter V?
5. What is the only MLB team that contains two S's?
6. What is the only MLB team that contains a double consonant?

ROCK-PAPER-SCISSORS HACKS

Players: 2

In Rock-Paper-Scissors, which dates back some 2,000 years to China's Han Dynasty, two players count to three, then simultaneously throw one of three shapes ("rock," "paper," "scissors") with an outstretched hand. Rock breaks scissors, scissors cut paper, and paper wraps rock. If both players throw the same shape, it's a tie... and they throw again.

People sometimes use Rock–Paper–Scissors to determine who's "It" in a game or to decide who has to take out the trash or some other task no one wants to do.

Here are a few hacks that players have made to this classic hand game.

BEAR-HUNTER-NINJA

This variant was popularized by a FedEx commercial.

Try this:

1. Aim an imaginary rifle and yell "Bang!"; you're a "hunter." Throw your arms in the air and growl; you're a "bear." Crouch and swing an imaginary *shinobigatana*; you're a "ninja."

2. Stand back to back with your opponent. At the count of three, whirl around and strike one of the game's three poses. Hunter shoots bear; bear eats ninja; ninja disarms hunter.

Illustrations by Mister Reusch

ROCK-PAPER-SCISSORS-LIZARD-SPOCK

A five-weapon variant, popularized by the TV show *Big Bang Theory*.

Try this:

1. Bring your fingertips together; this represents "lizard." Make the Vulcan salute (fingers parted between the middle and ring finger) from *Star Trek*; this represents "Spock." The hand gestures representing "rock," "paper," and "scissors" are the ordinary ones.

2. Scissors cuts paper. Paper covers rock. Rock crushes lizard. Lizard poisons Spock. Spock smashes scissors. Scissors decapitates lizard. Lizard eats paper. Paper disproves Spock. Spock vaporizes rock. Rock crushes scissors.

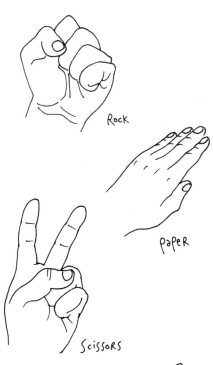

Rock

Paper

Scissors

TEETER-TOTTER

This variant is played standing up. Hopefully on a soft surface.

Try this:

1. Begin the game toe-to-toe. The players' right feet will never budge.

2. Each time you lose a throw, move your left foot back a step. And each time you win a throw, move your left foot forward a step (unless your left foot is already where it started).

3. The last player standing is the winner.

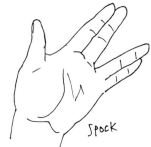

Spock

Lizard

BIRD-WATER-ROCK

This variant of the game hails from Singapore.

Try this:

1. Bring your fingertips together to form a beak; this represents "bird." Hold your hand out, palm up; this represents "water." A closed fist represents "rock," as usual.

2. Bird drinks water; stone hits bird; water sinks stone.

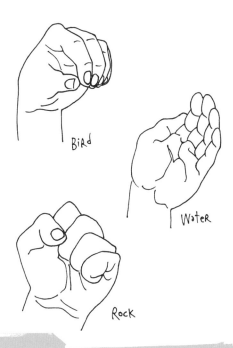

MINDGAME

Hidden Words:
BOARDGAMES

In 404 BC the Spartan naval commander, Lysander, defeated the Athenian fleet at the Battle of Aegospotami. He celebrated this momentous victory by picking grapes off a big bunch in front of his closest advisers, throwing them into the air one by one, and trying to catch them in his mouth. After he had dropped a few on the floor, he happened to look down and see that four of them were laid out in a perfectly straight diagonal line. This is how Connect 4 was invented. That's a complete lie, of course. But if you say it convincingly enough, you can get people to believe you.

The following six sentences are similarly sneaky when it comes to board games. Each one conceals the name of a popular game.

Can you find all six? Here's a seventh example that shows you just how sneaky sentences can be; the hidden board game is underlined: That's n**ot wister**ia! It's a maple tree that someone has painted purple.

1. Elmo! No polysyllabic words! Remember that they're only toddlers.
2. Will this crab blend in successfully with all the others? I'm worried about him.
3. My brain aches so badly that it makes my ears turn red.
4. War is known to be a very costly exercise.
5. Do you prefer biscuits or rye toast with your breakfast?
6. Huge electric arc as son nears high voltage generator; dad panics.

SPIT THE PIT

& OTHER BACKYARD CHALLENGES

Players: The more the merrier

In our first *Unbored* book, we wrote about ways to share your yard with friends and neighbors. Here are some more activities that are particularly great for outdoor parties.

SPIT THE PIT

You'll need:
- Lots of cherries (eat one, keep the pit in your mouth)
- A tarpaulin (tarp), or roll of paper, that's between 15' and 20' long
- Permanent marker
- Yardstick or tape measure

Illustrations by Mister Reusch

Try this:

1. Establish a Spit Line, and unroll the tarp or paper in front of it.

2. Using the tape measure or yardstick and permanent marker, draw a straight line the length of the tarp or paper. Then mark the line with feet and inches, moving away from the Spit Line.

3. On your turn, stand facing the tarp or paper roll—with your toes behind the Spit Line. Spit the cherry pit from your mouth as far as you can in front of you. You'll want to put your whole body into it: Puff your cheeks! Arch your back! Make that pit go as far as you can.

4. Once the pit has landed, circle it with the marker and write your name or initials next to the circle.

5. Keep taking turns, until everyone has gone three times. Whoever spat the farthest, wins.

REGGAE MUSICAL CHAIRS

You can spice up the classic birthday party game Musical Chairs by playing reggae, bluegrass, punk rock… or anything, really, that isn't music made for toddlers.

You'll need:
- Chairs, one per player.
- Loud music

Try this:

1. Arrange the chairs in a circle, the bigger the better.

➡ HACKS

Place one of the chairs—call it the "Satellite Chair of Death," perhaps— somewhere fairly far *outside* the circle. In each round, two players will have to rush for it as a last resort.

2. Appoint someone to be the music minder. Whenever the music is switched on, players begin walking around the circle. Whenever the music is switched off, players scramble to find a seat and sit down on it. Only one chair per person!

3. At the beginning of each round, remove one chair. When the music stops, whichever player can't find a seat is eliminated. When there's just one remaining chair, whoever sits in it when the music stops is the winner.

DOUGHNUT ON A STRING

You'll need:
- At least 1 doughnut per player
- Flat wrapping ribbon. Don't use string or thread, which will cut through the doughnut!
- Step ladder. Use with grownup supervision.

Try this:

1. Using the wrapping ribbon and step ladder, hang all the doughnuts—from a tree branch, perhaps, or a clothesline or a swing set with the swings temporarily removed. For each doughnut, the ribbon's length must be customized to

CARNIVAL GAMES

SQUIRT GUN SHOOTING GALLERY

You'll need:
- A 24" long piece of styrofoam
- 8 golf tees
- 8 ping pong balls
- A squirt gun or Super Soaker

Try this:

1. Press the golf tees into a straight line on the styrofoam, spaced 3" apart.

This is your shooting gallery; place it on a picnic or card table. Put a ping pong ball onto each tee.

2. Establish a shooting line—i.e., a place where players should stand when shooting. This can vary from player to player, depending on their age and ability. Make it challenging, though!

3. On your turn, fire one squirt of water at each ping pong ball. The player who knocks off the most balls wins. If more than one player knocks off all eight balls, then move the starting line back a foot, and try again. Repeat until one player knocks more balls of the tees than anyone else.

the player's height. Each player should be able to reach the doughnut with his mouth. (It's OK to make players stand on tiptoes, though, or squat.) Obviously, the ribbon should be threaded through the doughnuts' holes.

2. Position each player in front of the doughnut selected for them. Players must keep their hands clasped behind their backs at all times.

3. Have a grownup yell "Go!" The first person to eat an entire doughnut wins.

TOILET PAPER TOSS

You'll need:

- A clean toilet seat. If removing it from a toilet, use grownup supervision.
- Rope
- 4 rolls of toilet paper
- Duct tape

Try this:

1. Using the rope, hang the toilet seat—from a tree branch, perhaps, or a clothesline or a swing set with the swings temporarily removed, or a basketball hoop. There must be room on both sides of the toilet seat for an object to sail through... so don't hang it on a wall.

2. Wrap each roll of toilet paper with duct tape.

3. On your turn, standing at least 4' away from the hanging toilet seat, try to throw each roll of toilet paper through the seat—one at a time. Whoever scores the most "goals" wins that

round. If more than one player gets all four rolls through, then move the starting line back a foot, and try again. Repeat until one player scores more toilet-seat goals than anyone else.

COOPERATIVE

GAME
CHANGERS

TEAM
BUILDING

GAME THE SYSTEM!

By Stephen Duncombe

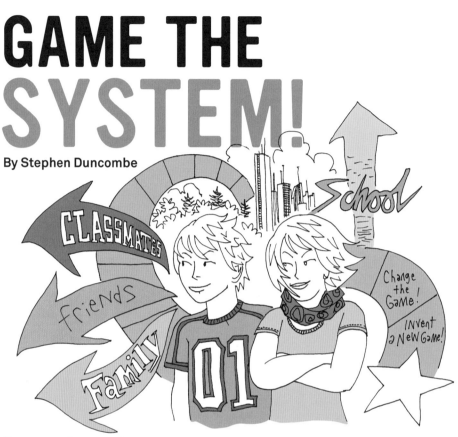

Every game has a goal, which provides you with a reason to keep playing. And every game has rules, which make reaching the goal a fun challenge. These things are true of life, too.

You belong to various communities: your family, neighborhood, school, city, state, maybe a religious or an ethnic community too. Each of those communities shares goals; and those goals are made difficult to reach by built-in, unavoidable obstacles that we might call "rules." As you compete and collaborate with others to achieve those goals, here are some pointers.

Play the Game

Whether you're playing field hockey, *Minecraft*, or convincing your school to start an anti-bullying campaign, the most important first step is figuring out how the system works and what's at stake.

Figure out the games you are playing and their contexts. You might play the Homework Game, for example, at the kitchen table every weekday from 4 p.m. until dinner. If you're someone who cares a lot about the environment, then perhaps you play the Green Game whenever you recycle, or encourage your grownups to use less energy, or reuse a container.

Illustrations by Mister Reusch

TOP 10 GAMES
FOR ACTIVISTS
By Stephen Duncombe

Monopoly
No other game demonstrates the brutal logic of the system of capitalism better.

Chess
You always need to think many steps ahead. That's good practice for planning activist strategy.

Battleship
Part of being an activist is trying to figure out what your opponent has planned, while keeping your own plans hidden.

Minecraft
The goal of all activism is to build a new world. *Minecraft* gives you a space to create (and battle creepers too).

Grand Theft Auto
Horrifically violent and politically incorrect. But sometimes it's OK to play a game without worrying about its politics.

Baseball
If you want to win over the majority of the people to your cause, you should understand what they like. Everyone likes baseball.

Role Playing Games
Part of being an activist is speaking up when you'd otherwise be quiet, or being bold when you are afraid, i.e., acting like someone you're not (yet).

Long Distance Running
Perseverance in the face of adversity—running, even though every muscle in your body is telling you to quit—is a good trait to have as an activist.

Whack-a-Mole
Just when you think you've won the game, another problem pops up.

Life
Not the boardgame *Life*, but the real thing: the biggest, best game of all.

Think about who you're playing with and against. What are your powers and limitations? What can your competitors do and not do? Who's on your team—and do they realize they're on your team?

Suss out each game's rules and goal. What "moves" can you make? Which actions get rewarded and which ones get penalized? How do you know if you're winning or losing the game?

Don't Play the Game
After analyzing the various games you play throughout the day, perhaps you've come to the conclusion that some of these games are rigged against you—that you'll never reach the goal no matter how hard you try. You might be tempted to stop trying so hard, to settle for failure. A riskier, but potentially more rewarding option, in such cases, is to refuse to play the game.

If your older sister encourages you to play basketball, then dominates you mercilessly on the court because you're smaller, complaining might not be as effective as going on strike. Refuse to play basketball, no matter how much she cajoles and insists. If you're determined not to participate in an unfair game, you might spark changes.

Friends

Change the Game

Quitting an unfair (or un-fun) game can sometimes lead to a revolution in the way that game is played. However, if quitting frees you from the game, but leaves the game unchanged, and others still have to play the game, then your decision to drop out might be more of a cop-out. If this seems to be the case, then your only option is to hang in there and fight for changes.

A game's rules—whether we're talking about baseball or how your family interacts—might seem permanent and natural. They're not. When you're playing a pick-up game of baseball with friends, and your outfielders have to go home for dinner, you invent a rule that will allow the game

to go on in a way that's fair: Any hit into the outfield, say, is an automatic double.

Remember: When you want to change the rules of a pick-up baseball game, you can't just announce the new rules. You have to huddle up, suggest ideas, and come to a consensus. Same thing applies to society's games. You'll need to negotiate and persuade.

Invent a New Game

We're all playing games, in everyday life, all the time. We can try to succeed within these game's existing rules, or quit altogether if we aren't satisfied by the games, or we can try to modify the rules to make the games more fun and fair. Or we can dream up bold new ways to play the Homework Game, the Green Game, the Family Game, and every other game in life.

If you were going to rewrite the Homework Game, perhaps you'd make a rule that lessons in math, history, and other topics would be learned at home in the evenings, at your kitchen table, by watching videos… and then during the school day, you'd do your homework in the classroom with your teacher's assistance. A few years ago, an educator named Sal Khan rewrote the Homework Game along those very lines; today, the "flipped classroom" is a growing trend.

So try imagining new and better ways to learn; to enjoy time with your family and friends to the fullest; to work for a greener planet or a world where fewer people are extremely rich or poor. What modifications to the existing rules of these games would be required? How would you go about persuading and motivating your fellow players to give your new rules a try?

In creating new games for living, we can change the world.

CO₂ SMACKDOWN!

Want to help fight climate change— while having fun? Check out these computer games and apps.

Go Green!

climatekids.nasa.gov/go-green/

NASA has created a bunch of computer games that explore different ways to protect the environment. *Go Green!* assigns transportation missions that you have to solve. For example, you might be babysitting your 4-year-old cousin at her house—and then need to take her to the park, a movie, and the toy store. Using a clickable map, you navigate the routes

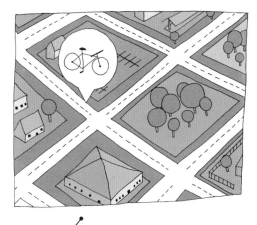

Go Green assigns you transportation missions that you have to solve with the least impact on the environment

Sort trash before it's too late in *Recycle This*

by choosing the method of transportation (bike, bus, car, carpool, on foot) that will both get you to your destination on time *and* have the least impact on the environment.

Solve your mission, and then take what you've learned out into the world.

Recycle This

climatekids.nasa.gov/recycle-this

Recycle This, another NASA game, depends on quick thinking and reflexes. You're sorting trash—that someone has tossed out a window, towards a garbage can—into the correct recycling bins before it's too late. If this sound too easy, keep in mind that every time you hold down your mouse button (which is how you sort the trash), you are using energy that drains the game's "battery." When you let go of the mouse, you recharge the battery… but the minute you do that, more trash falls! Surprisingly addictive for a simple educational game.

Green Up challenges you to "grow" seeds from around the world

Green Up

isygames.com/GreenUp_en.html

We all know that plants absorb greenhouse gases, right? In this game, you "grow" seeds from around the world into plants and trees. You need to figure out not only which seeds will thrive in different climates, but also how often they need to be watered and fertilized. You'll also have to protect your plants from pests and freezing temperatures.

Dumptown

epa.gov/recyclecity/gameintro.htm

How much waste can *you* save with programs that don't cost the city too much?

Dumptown has a serious trash problem. Not only are the streets littered with garbage, but the residents don't even recycle. In fact, everything they throw away ends up in a landfill. Developed by the U.S. Environmental Protection Agency, this challenging game turns you into Dumptown's newest city manager. You must not only convince residents to reuse and recycle, but also start new green-living programs—ranging from home composting to business recycling, to grass clipping services that help keep organic waste from polluting streams and rivers—all while making sure you don't spend over the town's budget.

Joulebug badges

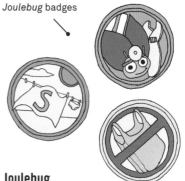

Joulebug

joulebug.com

With this social app, you and your family can compete against friends to see who will earn the most badges by making eco-friendly choices—from bringing a mug to the coffee shop to taking a shorter shower, to packing your lunch in reusable containers. What's more, your grownups can connect *JouleBug* to their utility accounts to see how much money your family saves by doing these tasks. Tell your grownups that the average player saves $200 a year!

GUERRILLA KINDNESS

Performing random acts of kindness is contagious—get in the game!

Players: The more the merrier

Want to encourage people to be kinder to each other? Want to discourage bullying? Try playing a couple of the following games.

GUERRILLA KINDNESS

Offer to help someone struggling with their bags at the grocery store. Pick up litter on the street. Thank your grownup for driving you everywhere, or thank a teacher for inspiring you. Performing random acts of kindness is contagious—especially if you turn it into a game. Invite friends to keep track of their kind acts during an assigned 24-hour period.

By the end, whoever has accomplished the most is the Guerrilla Kindness champ. Until next time, that is.

PS: You can also gamify your acts of kindness by purchasing *Boom Boom! Cards*, a kit containing 26 cards—each of which suggests a particular act of kindness. Your deck has a unique code, which you register at the website boomboomcards.com. After performing each act of kindness, log in and tell your fellow "agents of altruism" about it; then pass along that particular card to a friend. Via the website, you can track your friends' acts of kindness, too.

Illustration by Mister Reusch

CRUEL 2 B KIND

You'll need:
• At least one mobile phone per team
• **Optional:** Loot

Alternate reality game (ARG) designers Jane McGonigal and Ian Bogost dreamed up this twist on assassination-type games. Like those games, it requires a group of at least five people (the more the better), and it takes place in public spaces—like parks or entire neighborhoods. However, the goal of Cruel 2 B Kind (cruelgame.com) is to "kill" one another with kindness.

As in most ARGs, you'll need a game moderator (or "puppet master"), who sets the game's date and time and geographical boundaries, helps players remember the rules, and chooses each team's "weapons." The moderator—usually a grownup or teenager, because they'll need to communicate with players via telephone, email, and text messages—might decide, for example, that you can "assassinate" a target by blowing a kiss, pretending to mistake them for a celebrity, or paying them an outrageously nice compliment. Each time you successfully "kill" someone with kindness, you let the moderator know and they assign points.

Here's where things get really interesting. As in many other ARGs played in a public space, among a group of people who don't know one another well, *you might not know who your opponents are.* So you might end up complimenting or blowing a kiss to a random passerby. Which is the whole point of the game: spreading kindness, one person at a time.

Those are the game's basic rules. But there are lots of others, too, which the moderator can explain on game day. For example, each player might carry a prize (a comic book, a toy, whatever). If you're "killed," your assassin takes your prize. By the end of the game, successful assassins will be juggling an armful of loot. Another rule, which your game's moderator might or might not choose to apply: If you're "killed," instead of leaving the game you join the team of the player who did it to you… and keep on killing with kindness.

The game can end one of two ways. A "bloodbath" is where you keep playing for as long as it takes until one player, or one team, is left standing. Or the moderator can set a time limit—and when the time runs out, whichever player or team has earned the most points wins. Usually, everyone meets up after the game to share a few laughs, and perhaps to upload game photos to the Cruel 2 B Kind website.

You might compliment a random passerby

EXCUSE ME, JIMMY FALLON, COULD I PLEASE HAVE YOUR AUTOGRAPH?

Without looking at their card, each player sticks it to his or her own forehead

Treat someone more or less nicely according to the value of the card on his or her forehead

FACE VALUE

During our day-to-day lives, do we treat one another as nicely as we possibly could? Here's an easy card game—you can play it at school, or at a party—that gets players thinking about that question.

You'll need:

- A deck of cards
- Cellophane tape
- Timekeeper

Try this:

1. Deal one card, face-down, to each player. Each player then sticks a loop of tape to the back of his own card.

2. Without looking at their card, each player sticks it to their own forehead. The idea is that you can see the value of everyone else's card... but not your own. Don't tell other players the value of their cards.

3. Walk around the room and mingle. Treat players more or less nicely according to the value of the cards on their foreheads. If someone's card is a face card (Jack, Queen, King) or an ace, then behave as though they're really cool and you really want them to like you. If the value of someone's card is between 6 and 10, then be pleasant to them—but don't over-do it. If the value of someone's card is between 2 and 5, then you should try to avoid them. No need to be overtly cruel or nasty about it, but don't hang out with the low-value card players.

4. After five minutes, the timekeeper should call "Time!" Don't look at your card yet, and don't tell anyone the value of their card. Everyone should sort themselves into a group (high cards, middle cards, low cards), depending on how they feel they were treated by the other players.

5. Now look at the value of your card. Was it easy to figure it out? Discuss.

BEST EVER
COOPERATIVE BOARDGAMES

In games like *Forbidden Island*, players cooperate to win

Cooperative boardgames require some mental readjustment.

Your fellow players aren't your opponents; they're on your team! Either you all beat the game, or you all lose!

Lord of the Rings

Designed by Reiner Knizia
Each player takes on the role of one of five hobbits; the object of the game is to destroy the One Ring before the ring-bearer is captured by Sauron. During each turn, a player must flip Event Tiles—some of which cause bad events to happen to the hobbits, others of which cause good events to happen. Not to be confused with the children's game of the same name.
Players: 2–5 | **Age:** 12+
Duration: 60 minutes

Shadows Over Camelot

Designed by Bruno Cathala and Serge Laget
Each player is one of the knights of Camelot (or King Arthur himself), and together you defend ancient Britain from the forces of evil. The knights must defeat the Black Knight, search for Excalibur and the Holy Grail, and more. Meanwhile, catapults are surrounding Camelot.
Players: 3–7 | **Age:** 10+
Duration: 90 minutes

Pandemic

Designed by Matt Leacock
Diseases are breaking out around the world, and the game's players—each of whom is a disease-fighting specialist, such as an Operations Expert or a Scientist—must work closely together to eradicate them. Players travel around the world, from outbreak to outbreak.
Players: 2–4 | **Age:** 8+
Duration: 60 minutes

Forbidden Island
Designed by Matt Leacock

As adventurers move around an island—constructed from game tiles, in a different arrangement each time you play—it slowly sinks! You're on a mission to retrieve four treasures from the island before it vanishes beneath the waves. Each character has a special ability, so on your turn you'll want to consult with your teammates about what your best course of action might be.

Players: 2–4 | **Age:** 10+
Duration: 30 minutes.

Max
Designed by Jim Deacove

Since 1972, Family Pastimes has designed games in which people play together and not against each other. Some favorite games include *Amazing Illusions* (a team of magicians performs illusions—and tries not to get trapped in them) and *Mountaineering* (a group works together to scale a mountain). But even older players will enjoy simpler Family Pastime games, including *Caves & Claws*, *Harvest Time*, and particularly *Max*—in which players work together to distract a tomcat.

Players: 1–8 | **Age:** 4+
Duration: 20 minutes

Castle Panic
Designed by Justin De Witt

Do you enjoy the addictive online game/app *Kingdom Rush*? Here's a tower defense boardgame in which players work together to defend their castle against a horde of crazed trolls, goblins, orcs, and other monsters. Strategizing is important: If you have a card that won't be useful for battling monsters until it's another player's turn, then swap it for another card with that player. You're all in this mess together.

Players: 1–6 | **Age:** 8+
Duration: 60 minutes

MINDGAME

Hidden Words:
ZOO ANIMALS

Have you ever been to the zoo and seen no animals because they're all hiding in their caves, lairs, and hutches? It's enough to make you stay at home next time and watch animal videos on YouTube instead. But spare a thought for the furry and feathery ones. If you had hundreds of people peering through your bedroom window each day, you'd hide too. To celebrate the right of all zoo animals to hide from people if they want to, a different creature has been concealed in each of the six sentences to the right.

If you don't know how zoo animals go about hiding in words, the underlined part of the sentence below will show you:

Have you ever noticed how pathetic a melon looks when it's been left out in the rain?

1. Give me the password to your blog or I'll attack you.
2. Why enable the force field? It's a complete waste on the first level.
3. When I grow up I want to be a rollercoaster designer.
4. Why is my share portfolio not making me lots of money?
5. Bronze, brass and the exotic-sounding molybdochalkos are all alloys of copper.
6. Was Galileo pardoned? Or is he still considered a heretic?

ALASKAN
BASEBALL

Players: 8+

Here's a baseball-type game that doubles as a getting-to-know you exercise.

You'll need:
- A baseball—or tennis ball or any other baseball substitute
- A large open space

Try this:

1. Divide into two teams, and decide which team gets to go first. A player from the first team holds the baseball, while her teammates form a loose circle around her.

2. The player throws the baseball as far as she can, then begins to yell out the names of each member of her team—turning in a circle and pointing at each teammate. As soon as she has named everyone, she starts over and does it again, as many times as she can before the other team stops her. Each time she makes a complete circuit, her team scores one run.

3. Meanwhile, the other team chases the baseball. As soon as one player picks up the ball, the rest of his team forms a line behind him. The team members pass the ball along the line between

their legs... and then, once the last person in line receives the object, they pass the ball back to the head of the line—this time, over their heads. Once the ball returns to the first player in line, he yells "Stop!" and the other team stops naming names (and counting runs).

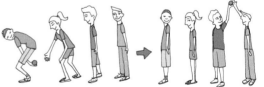

4. The player who retrieved the ball—and yelled "Stop!"—is circled by his teammates. He throws the ball as far as he can, then begins to turn in a circle, yelling out the names of his team. The other team scrambles to retrieve the ball, and so forth.

5. Repeat Steps 3 through 5 until each team has had five turns. Tally up your scores, and declare a winner.

Illustrations by Heather Kasunick

QB RESCUE

Players: 8+

Here is a version of football that doesn't involve tackling—but it gets you moving.

You'll need:

- Cones, or some other way of marking three long lines
- Five or more footballs or football substitutes
- A large open space
- **Optional:** A referee

Try this:

1. Mark a long straight line. On either side of that line, mark a long curved line. The playing field created by these lines should be oval-shaped, and at least 10' by 10' in area.

2. Divide into two teams, and elect one player from each team to be the starting quarterback (QB). The two QBs stand in the center of the field, facing each other across the straight line. Their teammates gather *behind* the curved lines—each team should be facing its own QB. The referee (if there is one) should now issue a football to each starting QB, then say "Go!"

3. The QBs throw to their own teammates. If a teammate catches the ball and successfully throws it back, then that player joins the QB on the field as another QB. But if the QB's pass to a teammate or the teammate's pass back to the QB is incomplete (dropped), then the QB must try again. Note: At any time, a QB may try to deflect or intercept a rival QB's pass! If one team ends up without any footballs, then its QBs *must* attempt to make interceptions.

4. As each new QB enters the playing field, she is issued a football (by a referee, if there is one). If there are no more footballs to issue, that's OK. You can always intercept a pass.

5. When every member of one team is on the field, then they have won the game.

THE GLAD GAME

AN EXCERPT FROM

POLLYANNA

by Eleanor H. Porter

The hero of Eleanor H. Porter's popular 1913 novel *Pollyanna* is a girl who goes to live with her stern Aunt Polly after her missionary father dies. The girl's optimistic attitude—demonstrated in this excerpt, where Pollyanna is talking to Aunt Polly's grumpy servant, Nancy—transforms the entire town. PS: In 1915, Parker Brothers created *The Glad Game*, based on the fictional Pollyanna's pastime.

"I—I'm afraid you'll have ter have bread and milk in the kitchen with me," [said Nancy]. "Yer aunt didn't like it—because you didn't come down ter supper, ye know."

"But I couldn't. I was up here."

"Yes; but—she didn't know that, you see!" observed Nancy, dryly, stifling a chuckle. "I'm sorry about the bread and milk; I am, I am."

"Oh, I'm not. I'm glad."

"Glad! Why?"

"Why, I like bread and milk, and I'd like to eat with you. I don't see any trouble about being glad about that."

"You don't seem ter see any trouble bein' glad about everythin'," retorted Nancy, choking a little over her remembrance of Pollyanna's brave attempts to like the bare little attic room.

Pollyanna laughed softly.

"Well, that's the game, you know, anyway."

"The—*game*?"

"Yes; the 'just being glad' game."

"Whatever in the world are you talkin' about?"

"Why, it's a game. Father told it to me, and it's lovely," rejoined

Pollyanna. "We've played it always, ever since I was a little, little girl. I told the Ladies' Aid, and they played it—some of them."

"What is it? I ain't much on games, though."

Pollyanna laughed again, but she sighed, too; and in the gathering twilight her face looked thin and wistful.

"Why, we began it on some crutches that came in a missionary barrel."

"Crutches!"

"Yes. You see I'd wanted a doll, and father had written them so; but when the barrel came the lady wrote that there hadn't any dolls come in, but the little crutches had. So she sent 'em along as they might come in handy for some child, sometime. And that's when we began it."

"Well, I must say I can't see any game about that," declared Nancy, almost irritably.

"Oh, yes; the game was to just find something about everything to be glad about—no matter what 'twas," rejoined Pollyanna, earnestly. "And we began right then—on the crutches."

"Well, goodness me! I can't see anythin' ter be glad about—gettin' a pair of crutches when you wanted a doll!"

Pollyanna clapped her hands.

"There is—there is," she crowed. "But I couldn't see it, either, Nancy, at first," she added, with quick honesty. "Father had to tell it to me."

"Well, then, suppose *you* tell *me*," almost snapped Nancy.

"Goosey! Why, just be glad because you *don't—need—'em!*" exulted Pollyanna, triumphantly. "You see it's just as easy—when you know how!"

"Well, of all the queer doin's!" breathed Nancy, regarding Pollyanna with almost fearful eyes.

"Oh, but it isn't queer—it's lovely," maintained Pollyanna enthusiastically. "And we've played it ever since. And the harder 'tis, the more fun 'tis to get 'em out; only—only sometimes it's almost too hard—like when your father goes to Heaven, and there isn't anybody but a Ladies' Aid left."

"Yes, or when you're put in a snippy little room 'way at the top of the house with nothin' in it," growled Nancy.

Pollyanna sighed.

"That was a hard one, at first," she admitted.

Referees walk about acting as "disease"

SURVIVE!
PREDATOR & PREY

Players: 10+, the more the merrier

Predator and Prey combines elements of tag and a scavenger hunt to simulate the rules of the food chain in the natural world. Some players are predators, the others are prey.

The game is best played in the woods or a park where you have plenty of room to run and find hidden objects. We asked the staff of Camp Widjiwagan (in Ely, Minnesota) for pointers.

You'll need:

- A bandanna per player
- 3 whistles (one for each predator pack)
- A bell or noise-making device, for the referee
- 4 food markers (wood, or laminated paper, marked with an "F")
- 4 shelter markers (wood, or laminated paper, marked with an "S")

Referee

Before the game begins, choose someone as the referee. This person will designate the playing area's boundaries, hide the food and shelter markers (no peeking!), keep time during the game, and act as "Disease." The referee should go over the rules with all players.

Try this:

1. Divide into groups. You'll need three predator packs: one wolf pack, with no fewer than 2 or 3 members; and two fox packs, with no fewer than 2 or 3 members apiece. Every other player is a vole—that is, a mouse-like rodent. Use your bandanna to show which type of animal you are. If you're a vole, wear the bandanna as a headband; if you're a fox, wear the bandanna as an armband; if you're a wolf, wear the bandanna sticking out of a pocket. One player in each of the three predator packs is designated that pack's Brain; the Brain is issued a whistle.

2. The referee signals for the voles to scatter. A minute or so later, the referee releases the foxes. And a minute or so after that, the referee rings the bell—which signals that the wolves have been released. If you are a wolf,

your pack can hunt for foxes and voles; if you are a fox, your pack can hunt for voles, and can be hunted by wolves. If you are a vole, you can be hunted by wolves and foxes. Voles can cooperate, but they are not a pack with a Brain.

3. In order to survive the winter, before the referee rings the bell again (signaling the game's end), each wolf pack must gather 3 foods and 1 shelter; each fox pack must gather 2 foods and 1 shelter; and each vole must gather 1 food and 1 shelter. You "gather" food and shelter by seeking out the markers hidden earlier by the game's referee.

> **IMPORTANT:** Leave the markers where they are, so that other players can find them. Each vole keeps tracks of how many markers he's found; each Brain keeps track of how many markers her pack has found.

We Need to catch at least 3 More Voles to survive the Winter

Foxes

4. In addition to locating hidden markers, wolf and fox packs have another means of gathering food: by hunting. If you're a wolf or fox, and your pack's Brain blows her whistle, then you have 10 seconds in which to "run and chase." While your Brain counts loudly to 10, the pack scatters—they're not allowed to go more than 30' from the Brain, though—and attempts to tag other players. After counting to 10, the Brain blows her whistle twice—and all pack members must immediately return to the Brain and huddle up. Any tagged foxes or voles join the wolf pack; they should immediately switch their bandanna to represent their new pack affiliation.

5. Here are a few game guidelines. A pack's Brain is invincible, and can't be hunted. Remember that while wolves and foxes can both tag voles, only wolves can tag foxes—and wolves can't be tagged. In order to gather 1 food unit, a wolf pack must tag 4 foxes or voles; and a fox pack needs to tag 3 voles. After each hunt, the pack's huddle allows the Brain to figure out how many resources the pack has gathered; the huddle also gives the pack's un-tagged prey in the vicinity a sporting chance to flee.

6. As if all this searching for markers and hunting prey weren't chaotic enough, the referee walks around acting as "Disease." If a wolf or fox pack grows unfairly huge, then the referee will select members of that pack and announce that they've been killed by disease. (They become voles.) You're not allowed to run from the referee; disease is inescapable.

WOLF PACK

7. After 45 or 60 minutes, the referee rings the bell to announce the end of the game. Now it's time to find out which players have survived the winter. Are you a member of a fox or wolf pack that's less than half the size it was when the game began? Sorry, you didn't survive. Are you a vole or predator pack that didn't gather enough food and shelter? Sorry, you didn't survive, either. However, if you're a vole who did gather enough food and shelter, or a predator pack who gathered enough food and shelter *and* is at least half as large as you were at the game's beginning, then congratulations! You survived—and you won the game.

MINDGAME

Anagrams:
HARRY POTTER CHARACTERS

Anagrams are powerful weapons for humiliating people. If you ever find yourself in an argument with Arnold Schwarzenegger, for example, you will be able to silence him by pointing out that the letters in his name can be arranged to spell "He's grown large 'n' crazed." Similarly if Justin Timberlake cuts in front of you at the supermarket, you can bring his cheeks out in the rosiest blush by announcing loudly to all the other customers that rudeness is hardwired into his name. It surely can't be a coincidence that Justin Timberlake is an anagram of "I'm a jerk. But listen." Not all name anagrams need be humiliating, though; some can be downright surreal.

Take the six strange phrases below. Can you rearrange the letters in each one to give the name of a Harry Potter character?

1. Soluble Beard Mud
2. Enraging Her More
3. Bushier Guard
4. Suaveness Rep
5. Love Bottling Lemon
6. Calm Loving Manager

CHILL!
STRESS-RELIEVING GAMES

Players: 1+

Does your body ever feel like it's an engine kicking into high speed? Do you worry a lot about stuff like tests, playing a musical solo, or whether or not your best friend is mad at you?

If you answer Yes to any of these questions, you could be stressed out. (It's OK! Most of us are, from time to time.) Playing any game in this book is a great way to relax, because games take your mind off whatever is bugging you. The following games, however, are specially designed to help you chill out. You can play most of these on your own, but feel free to include friends and family.

Cloudspotting

Go outside and look into the sky. Pick a cloud that is shaped like an object from the real or imagined world—a horse, for example, or a hobbit, or a hammer. Watch this object until the cloud disappears. Then spot something new and do it all over again.

Line Up

Pick an object or scene and draw it—without picking up your pencil. Make it as detailed as you like, just as long as the pencil point never leaves the paper. This is a good game to play with friends because the results are usually hilarious… and laughing is a great stress-buster.

Illustrations by Mister Reusch

High Count

Sit down, close your eyes and see how high you can count until your mind wanders. Most of us have a hard time making it to 10! Do it again, only this time try to beat your previous score. If it's a challenge to stay focused, don't worry. Take a few deep breaths, notice that your mind is starting to stray and gently redirect your attention back to the numbers.

Meditation Flowers

zefrank.com/meditation_flowers/

A lot of videogames—*Minecraft*, anyone?—might seem relaxing. In fact, many videogames *increase* stress… because you get so absorbed that you feel like you can't stop playing. An online videogame that truly helps you chill out is *Meditation Flowers*. Hum or sing to make the flower pattern on the screen spin and change shape. Do higher notes or louder sounds make the pattern move more quickly? There are no winners or losers in this game. There are no scores, either.

Silent Ball

Physical activity is a great way to relax. The object of Silent Ball is to keep the ball in play without making any noise. No talking. No laughing. Be quiet!

Try this:

1. Get a group of people together and stand in a circle. Choose one person to be the referee. This person can still play, but they're also allowed to talk—when calling someone out.

2. The referee tosses the ball—easily—to someone, to get things started. On your turn, you simply catch the ball and toss it to someone else. The referee will call you out if you…

    • talk or make any sound
    • drop the ball
    • toss the ball too high or too low, or too fast, for someone to catch it
    • toss the ball back to the person who tossed it to you

3. The last two people standing are the winners. But everyone wins, because they're relaxed.

Meditation Flowers is a videogame that truly helps you chill out

CIRCLE OF
DOOM

I added some mayo.... a couple pickles..... and ... some... CHEESE!

Players: 5+

A break-the-ice game should meet the following criteria. 1) Participants can easily join or leave without affecting the outcome of the game. 2) The instructions are simple. 3) You don't need any specialized skill. This game fits the bill.

Try this:

1. Select the game's Story-Teller.

2. All other players form a circle around the Story-Teller. Players should stand at arm's length from one another.

3. Stretch out your arms. Hold your left hand flat, palm facing upward. With your right hand, point your index finger down into the open palm of the player to your right. Your finger should be hovering slightly over that player's open palm; and the player to your left's finger should be hovering slightly over your open palm.

4. The story-teller announces a keyword, which—when spoken by the story-teller—will serve as a signal for everyone to attempt to snap closed

their left hand (around a player's finger), while simultaneously jerking their right hand away (from a player's closing hand).

5. Here's an example. The story-teller tells a story about building a perfect sandwich; and the keyword is *cheese*. "I went to the grocery store, where I bought some lettuce, mayo... and *cheese*." [Chaos as everyone grabs with their left hand and jerks away their right hand; then everyone returns to the starting position.] "Back at my house, I cut two slices of wheat bread. I spread the mayo onto the bread. I also put some mustard, and salt and pepper onto the bread. Then I placed one single leaf of lettuce on the sandwich... plus a slice of *cheese*."

6. That's it! There are no winners and losers in this game, it's just for laughs.

Illustration by Mister Reusch

NINJA WAH!

Players: 6+

Bunny Bunny originated in the 1950s as an inhibition-shedding exercise for improv (improvisational) theater actors. Since then, it has evolved into a ninja-themed circle game.

Try this:

1. Stand in a circle facing each other. Decide which player starts.

2. The starting player raises her arms over her head, with palms together, and says, "Wah!"

3. The two players on either side of her become ninjas. Placing their own palms together, they simultaneously make a chopping motion aimed at the waist of the player who said "Wah!" Note: They do not actually touch their victim. However, they are allowed to make ninja noises.

4. The victim of the ninjas quickly bends forward at the waist, keeping her palms together, and points her fingers at at any player *except* one

of the two ninjas who just chopped her. (Making eye contact with the new victim is important, so he gets the message.) The player to whom she points immediately raises his arms over his head, with palms together, and says, "Wah!" The two players on either side of him become ninjas, and so forth.

5. The game continues in that fashion— as quickly as possible—until a player makes a mistake (performs the wrong motion, does not say "Wah!") or hesitates. That player then steps out of the circle, and the game continues. While the game goes on, any eliminated players walk around, distracting other players by heckling them—though without touching or yelling.

6. Once all but four of the players in the circle have been eliminated, the game is over. The four remaining players are the winners.

Videogames challenge gamers to think and act quickly and creatively.

Massively multiplayer online role-playing games allow gamers to bond with a team.

5 soup gravy beans

Alas, real life is rarely so packed with excitement and opportunities for teamwork.

CO2:380 PPM   °C:57 $8   0

Menu   next Impact: 400   2000

After every 387 downloads, World Bicycle Relief donates a new bike to a child in need.

Recently, "serious" games have emerged. They educate gamers about world issues.

The app CLIMATE DEFENSE, for example, asks you to prevent global warming by either decreasing carbon dioxide emissions or increasing the efficiency of energy consumption.

Other apps like the bike-racing game SIDEKICK CYCLE have a real-world impact.

▷ Serious ARGs (Alternate Reality Games) challenge you to hack the real world. For example, in 2008, the game SUPERSTRUCT asked players to imagine the problems of the year 2019 then figure out solutions.

I ♥ Bees

SUPERSTRUCT was organized by Jane McGonigal, who had the brilliant idea to take the gamer's way of thinking and acting... and use these things for real-world good.

McGonigal realized that ARGs could combine fun experience and serious purpose. Now her games—

EVOKE

SUPERBETTER

world without oil

☀CRUEL 2 B KIND☀

—encourage players to tackle real-world problems, be kind to strangers, and increase physical activity.

Mr. Scott, AP Enviro Sci. teacher, USA

ARGs are catching on! For example: An environmental studies ARG called THE BLACK CLOUD challenged students to test and improve the air quality in their schools.

PUFF

The ARG Manifesto
1. Think big. Gamers enjoy feeling part of something larger than themselves. 2. Foster community. Gamers love making connections with one another. 3. Gamers are mentally tough and emotionally resilient; they know that failure is a great way to learn. 4. Remember that it's a game — so have fun!

Let's see how many pollinated foods we can find. For every five foods, we'll donate $1.00 to the Xerces Society for pollinator preservation.

Not ready to design a game for others? Begin by gamifying your own life.

HUNGER GAMES

Can gaming be a part of the solution to urgent social problems like hunger, poverty, disease, conflict, climate change, and sustainable energy?

The World Bank Institute thinks so. In 2010, it launched EVOKE, an online "serious" (or "social impact") game meant to empower young people to collaborate with each other. And that's just one of several examples. Here are some favorites.

A CRASH-COURSE IN CHANGING THE WORLD

EVOKE
urgentevoke.com
Directed by Jane McGonigal, who designs "alternate reality" games intended to improve real lives or solve real problems, EVOKE was played via social media by kids in Africa for ten weeks. The game's players scored points by educating themselves about problems facing their own communities, sharing ideas with one another, then trying out innovative solutions.

3rd World Farmer
3rdworldfarmer.com
Players in the simulation game *3rd World Farmer* don't directly work to alleviate real-world problems. However, they learn how difficult it is to manage a farm in a developing nation while coping with drought, disease, corrupt government, and civil war. **Age: 13+**

Freerice
freerice.com
You, too, can play games that help alleviate hunger around the world. *Freerice*, for example, is a trivia game, with over 20 categories (e.g., famous paintings, world landmarks, English vocabulary, chemical symbols). For each question that you answer correctly, *Freerice* donates rice to the United Nations World Food Programme. **Age: 14+, unless you have a grownup's permission.**

Illustrations by Heather Kasunick

TRICK
YOUR MIND

You might imagine that you're making decisions in an entirely rational way. However, you're influenced by how choices are presented to you. We all are.

Illustrations by Heather Kasunick

For example, if you're craving an ice cream sundae and your grownup is willing to buy it, then you will likely decide to eat one; but if you know that you'd have to buy that sundae with your own money, then the fruit bar at the back of the freezer might suddenly look much yummier.

The study of how people's decisions—including your own—can be influenced goes by many names, including "behavioral economics" and "choice architecture." But let's just call it "tricking people's minds so they make one decision instead of another." In other words, you can treat choices and decisions like games, using strategies based on how the mind works.

This may sound sinister, but mind trick games can be used for good purposes, For example: Researchers have discovered that moving a cafeteria's salad bar front and center—near the cash register, say—can increase the sale of salads by 50 percent. Want to encourage kids to buy more white milk, and less sugary chocolate- and strawberry-flavored

milk? Try putting the chocolate and strawberry milk behind the white milk on the refrigerator shelf—it works!

If you're interested in improving the way you or your peers behave, try these mind games.

Take the high road

Whether you're selling Girl Scout cookies or raising money for your school, plant yourself at the top of an escalator instead of at the bottom. Researchers have found that twice as many mall shoppers who had just ridden an up escalator contributed to the Salvation Army than shoppers who had just ridden the down escalator. In another study by the same team, people watched film clips of scenes taken either from an airplane above the clouds or through the window of a passenger car. Participants who had watched the clip of flying above the clouds were 50 percent more cooperative (in a computer game which they played after watching the clip) than those who had watched the car ride on the ground.

What do escalators and flying have to do with being generous and cooperative? Researchers suspect that our brains may unconsciously associate height with behaving well; for example, when we say that we "look up" to someone, it means we respect them. Because height and good qualities are connected in our mind, when we're high off the ground we may be more inclined to behave in a generous, cooperative way.

A super-spicy way to break a bad habit

Gross yourself out

If you've got a bad habit you want to break, try making the habit so unpleasant that your brain will scream "stop" the next time you try it. A great example of this technique is "no bite" nail polish, which tastes so disgusting that nail biters eventually stop their chomping. You can also try hypnotizing yourself—for example, telling yourself over and over that soda pop tastes gross and makes you sick.

Invent a sales slogan

When a school cafeteria labeled carrots "X-ray vision carrots," sales of the normally unpopular veggie spiked by 50 percent. That's the power of suggestion in action. When advertisers play these kinds of games, we don't like it. But if your little sister hates bedtime, it can't hurt to invent a new, more appealing term for it, such as "snuggle time." If that same little sister doesn't like eating broccoli, try renaming the broccoli "trees," then tell her that she's a dinosaur, and beg her not to eat all the trees.

Invite peer pressure

If you have a goal you want to achieve— running a mile, maybe, or saving up to buy a snowboard—research shows that telling friends and family what your goal is, and then checking in with them every week to report on your progress (via an email, or photographs or even a video documenting how far you've come) will help you get there. There are lots of online and smartphone apps to help you check in with your support team.

Label it

Even though we all know that leaving the lights on and neglecting to unplug our tech chargers sucks up energy, it's difficult for grownups to change their habits. Try posting signs that say "CO2" above light switches, or drawing leaky faucets with $$ symbols on signs posted near the shower; that should get your grownups' attention. And if they're fed up with boys spraying pee all around the toilet, then they can try a labelling trick of their own. Using a red permanent marker, they can write "AIM" on a sticker and put it inside the toilet bowl. This strategy works wonders.

Turn peeing accurately into a game

MINDGAME

WHAT'S NEXT?

Until a couple of centuries ago, people stumbled through life trying and mostly failing to be understood. Only letters existed; words had yet to be invented. Homes, shops and parks were full of people shouting random consonants and vowels at each other in a vain attempt to convey their thoughts and wishes. And then one day in 1814 things changed. Some bright American spark realized you could combine all these letters in an infinite number of ways and began shouting words instead. Gone were the exasperated wails of "Z!", "B!" and "F!". Now the air was rich with cheerful bellows of "Trumpet!", "Compliance!" and

"Rhinoplasty!" To honor the 200th anniversary of this lexical revolution, you are invited to apply your mind to the following sequences of letters.

Now, while these sequences appear utterly meaningless, in a nod to the nonsense that once prevailed, they actually aren't. Can you figure out the significance of each sequence and hazard a guess at what should replace the question marks? If you're as confused as an 18th century letter-shouter, here's an example:

M, T, W, T, F, S, ? (Answer: S. Sunday is the last day in the series.)

1. J, F, M, A, M, J, J, A, S, O, N, ?
2. O, T, T, F, F, S, S, E, N, ?
3. S, M, H, D, W, M, ?
4. M, V, E, M, J, S, U, ?
5. TPM, AOTC, ROTS, ANH, TESB, ?
6. HPATSS, HPATCOS, HPATPOA, HPATGOF, HPATOOTP, HPATHBP, ?

THE WORLD'S GAME

Q&A with Tony Sanneh

Tony Sanneh racked up impressive accomplishments as a soccer pro—playing for D.C. United, Columbus Crew, and Los Angeles Galaxy, and representing the USA in the 2002 FIFA World Cup. But the goal he cares about most today is using the game of soccer to help improve kids' lives.

Former soccer pro Tony Sanneh in Haiti.

We talked to Tony about the Haitian Initiative (thesannehfoundation.org/haitian-initiative), a program that his Sanneh Foundation has developed. It gives kids in Haiti a reason to stay in school and become leaders.

UNBORED: How did you get started playing soccer?

SANNEH: I grew up in Minnesota, but my dad is from Gambia. When I was 6, I went to Africa to visit my family and all the boys on the street played soccer—so I went out and picked it up. There is no language barrier with soccer. Playing the game gave me a way to be accepted into the neighborhood quickly, and be part of a team.

UNBORED: How did you come up with the idea for Haitian Initiative?

SANNEH: After the earthquake in 2010, I went to Haiti as a member of the LA Galaxy to volunteer by teaching soccer and delivering supplies. We thought we'd run two or three soccer clinics a day, but because the kids wouldn't go in buildings—they were so scared of another earthquake and there was no school—they felt safer outdoors. So we ran clinics all day.

When we talk about basic needs, we think about food, shelter, and love. But my experience in Haiti made me realize that it's also a basic need, especially in times of grief, to play—to be allowed to be a child. Everything around these Haitian kids was serious and devastating. But for those moments they were on the field, the kids were able to escape… and be kids.

Photo courtesy Sanneh Foundation

That trip got me thinking about what I could do to help. So today our organization, which is run with partners in Haiti, teaches soccer 52 weeks a year—and also provides meals and health care to our players. To be in our program, Haitian kids are required to stay in school and do service projects.

UNBORED: Does playing soccer help kids in your program expand their horizons?

SANNEH: Yes. Indirectly, because they're encouraged to stay in school. Directly, because we bring one team every summer to Minnesota. They stay with host families, make friends, and grow as leaders. It's a multicultural mix of people being competitive and having fun.

UNBORED: Do the American kids who host them and play against them benefit?

SANNEH: They, who have so much, see kids who have so little enjoying life. And it's a gift to be able to give, to see that you can have a positive effect on another kid's life.

UNBORED: Soccer promotes fierce competition between teams and even countries. Why do you think that it can promote global understanding?

SANNEH: Soccer has been called "the world's game." It's often brought people together—there have even been wartime soccer games played during cease-fires. It's an inclusive game, because all you need to be able to do is run and kick. When you're playing soccer, you don't see differences on the field—you just see other players.

MINDGAME

Anagrams:
LOTR CHARACTERS

The Lord of the Rings trilogy is a sprawling epic. The whole enterprise is the long, and enjoyable, brainwave of an English genius, John Ronald Reuel Tolkien. But engage in a thought experiment for a moment. Can you imagine how much longer and weirder the trilogy would have been if all the characters had used anagrams of their names instead of their real names? "You're looking for Gandalf? I can't help you, sorry. The only wizard I know is called Dan Flag." "I thought Sauron was supposed to be the evil overlord of Mordor. You're telling me that it's now USA Ron?" "What do you mean Gollum's run off to open a novelty drinkware store called LOL Mugs?"

In this alternate Tolkienian universe, can you divine which LOTR characters might go by the following pseudonyms?

1. Gains Big Blob
2. Ring Keeper Too
3. Goofing Bards
4. Sewage Gas Mime
5. Maniac Drubbed Rocky
6. General Legal Foes

GAMIFY YOUR
FAVORITE CAUSES

If you've ever competed against other kids to raise the most money for your school, then you already know that playing a game is one of the most effective ways to support a good cause.

Why stop with helping out your school? Here are a few ways that you and your grownup can gamify the charities and other causes about which your family cares.

Chore scores

Gather with your family on a Sunday and make the following decisions. First, decide how much money your family will donate to charity at the end of the next three-month period. Each member of the household should then identify a charity to which she would like that money to

go, *and* a special reward that she'd really enjoy that week. PS: Everyone should pick a different charity; the idea is to get some friendly competition going.

Next, make a list of which chores need doing during the week ahead—and how many points each is worth. For example, loading the dishwasher might be worth 1 point, while picking up dog poop in the yard is worth 5 points.

When Sunday rolls around again, tally up that week's points and award the top scorer the prize they wanted. And at

Illustrations by Mister Reusch

Week 33	Ryan	Hunter	Anne	Joe
Load dishwasher 1 point	4	1	2	1
Fold Laundry 2 points	2		6	2
Collect Recycleables 3 points		3	3	9
Take out Trash 4 points				8
Pick up Dog poop 5 points	10		5	5
Mow Lawn 6 points				6

the end of the three-month period, tally up your cumulative scores. If you're the top scorer during the entire three-month period, then your family should make a donation to the charity or cause you picked at the beginning of the game.

If you keep playing this game, by the end of the year your family (or classmates, or friends) will have donated to charity four times—which is awesome.

Change combat

Issue each member of the family a jar of approximately the same size. Each member of the household should then identify a special reward that he'd really enjoy that month. And the entire family (or class, or school) should agree on a single charity or good cause to support.

The game begins on the first day of each month. The goal is to accumulate the most pennies before the end of the month—each penny in your jar is worth 1 point. Here's the tricky part: Each nickel, dime, or quarter that ends up in your jar

costs you 1 point! So during the game, put as many pennies as you can into your own jar, and as many silver coins as you can into your opponents' jars. At the end of the month, tally up your points.

Did you win? Then you've earned your special reward. Now put all the change together and donate it to the charity identified by your family at the beginning of the month. And start over.

USE APPS TO
MAKE CHANGES

Chore Wars

chorewars.com is an online RPG game that rewards you with "experience points" for recruiting a party of "adventurers" and competing to accomplish household chores.

Skills for Change

skillsforchange.com makes it easy for busy families to help good causes by "microvolunteering." After you identify causes your family cares about, you and your grownup will answer questions about your skills. The app will then direct you to challenges—big jobs, broken into smaller tasks—that you can accomplish quickly and easily.

NeighborGoods

neighborgoods.net is an online community service where your family can help your neighbors—and help the environment—by loaning out stuff you don't use every day, whether it's a lawnmower or a ladder. The site tabulates how much money you've saved (and helped your neighbors save) by sharing. Set a goal and watch your score rise.

EXPERIMENTATION

4

EXPLORATION

DUCT TAPE
ADVENTURE!

By Richela Fabian Morgan

Using mostly duct tape, my family and I created a portable boardgame, the setting of which is our own neighborhood. Its goal—walking to the local mini-mart and buying a snack—is something that my kids do on their own.

The point of our game, which we call *Go Get a Snack!,* is that adventure awaits whenever you step outside your door. Want to make a duct-tape game in which you'll explore your own neighborhood?

Start by thinking of a local adventure that you enjoy—or would like to enjoy. Then follow these instructions.

You'll need:

Duct Tape
- 1 roll of grass pattern
- 1 roll of black
- 5 21" lengths of silver
- 2 2" lengths of white
- A few dozen 1¼" lengths of various colors and patterns (other than silver, white, or grass)

Additional

- Dice and game pieces, which can be salvaged from other boardgames.
- Play money (or money you make yourself)
- A sheet of parchment paper, 15"x20"
- 10 5"x3" index cards
- Scissors
- A 24" ruler
- A pen
- A protractor or T-square (optional)
- A utility knife. Use with grownup supervision.
- Worktable

Create the game mat

1. Cut 9 23" lengths of grass-pattern tape. With the 15"x20" sheet of parchment paper in the "landscape" position, place the first strip of grass-pattern tape along the bottom edge of the paper. The bottom edge of the duct tape strip should overlap the bottom edge of the parchment paper by approximately ¼"; and the duct tape strips should stick out over the left and right sides of the parchment paper by approximately 1½".

2. Now add the other eight strips of grass-pattern tape, one at a time. The bottom edge of each new strip should overlap the top edge of the previous one by approximately ¼" (Figure A).

3. The edges of your game mat will be stuck to your worktable. Gently peel the mat off the table at one of the bottom corners, then pull upward in a diagonal direction until it's unstuck (Figure B). Flip the mat over, so the parchment paper side is face up. Peel off the paper (Figure C).

4. Cut 9 23" lengths of black tape. Using the same method you used in Step 2, cover the sticky side of your game mat with the black tape. Then flip the mat back to its grass-pattern side.

5. Using the 24" ruler and pen, plus (optional) a protractor or T-square for the corners, draw a rectangle that is slightly smaller than your game mat. Using the utility knife, and the ruler as a cutting guide, cut along the edges of this rectangle—to get rid of the game mat's sticky edges. Your game mat is now neat and tidy and ready to be designed (Figure D).

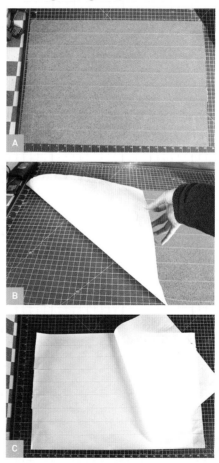

Design the game board

1. Cut 5 21" lengths of silver tape. With the mat's grass-pattern side face up, place these strips of tape onto the mat in evenly spaced rows. There should be at least ½" between the rows (Figure E). The silver tape represents the path you'll travel in the game. To create Start and Finish squares (at the game board's bottom left and top right), cut 2 2" lengths of white tape.

2. Next, add the game board's Action squares—the 1¼" lengths of tape, which can be any color or pattern other than grass, silver, or white. As you can see from our game, along each "street" we placed one or two gold squares, two skull & crossbones squares, between one and three animal-paw squares, and (randomly) several other patterns too. Finally, we used very thin strips of black tape to break up some long stretches of silver into multiple squares—and to create arrows connecting the "street" segments (Figure F).

Finished! The fun thing about using duct tape is that your game board is very portable. If you're going on a trip, for example, you can roll it up and stick it in your backpack.

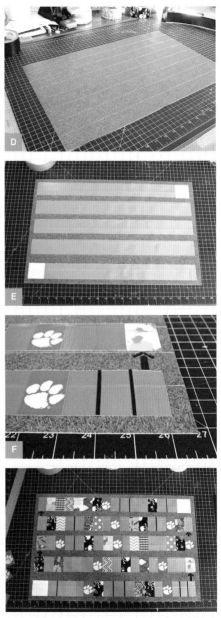

Once you've built your duct tape game board, it's time to invent the game's rules.

Invent game rules

Here are the rules for *Go Get a Snack!*. We used play money, dice, and game pieces scavenged from other boardgames we own. We wrote instructions on index cards; each card tells you how to obtain money—for example, "Take $5 from the player on your left."

Use the game board you've designed to make a game about an adventure in your own community. Our game is pretty simple—feel free to invent rules that are more complex!

1. Players begin at Home (represented by the white square at the board's bottom left). Each player has $20. The goal is to be the first to reach our neighborhood's mini-mart (represented by the white square at top right) with at least $5 left, for a snack. If you reach the Finish square without at least $5, then you must go back 20 spaces.

2. On your turn, roll two six-sided dice and move your game piece that number of spaces.

Here's how our Action Squares work:

- Silver = You are safe.
- Gold = Move ahead to the next gold space. If you are on the game board's last gold space, then you move ahead to the mini-mart.
- Skull & crossbones = Uh-oh! Move back to the last skull & crossbones space. If you land on the first skull & crossbones space, then you go back to Home.
- Animal paw print = Draw one card, which tells you how to obtain more money.
- Various colors/prints = You have landed on a local business. Subtract $3 from your total.

Scavenge play money, dice, and game pieces from other boardgames.

ROCKET RACING

Players: 2+

The object of this game is to blast a paper rocket into the sky, calculate the maximum altitude that it reaches, then challenge your friends—and yourself—to build an even better rocket.

First, you'll build an air-pressurized rocket launcher made from PVC and other hardware store items. With some grownup supervision and assistance, this activity should only take a few hours… however, you should allow the cement to set overnight before using the rocket launcher.

Before you head out to gather all the necessary parts and equipment, take a look at the lists of parts and equipment (facing page) that you'll need for building rockets and the inclinometer.

CAUTION! Although the PVC should be more than strong enough to withstand the 45 psi used for this project, exposure to sunlight, cold temperatures, or other damage could cause it to shatter. Grownup supervision is a must.

Illustration by Mister Reusch

Gather parts & equipment

You'll need the following PVC (Schedule 40) parts. Note that a *coupling* is a part that joins two pipes from the outside, while a *bushing* joins two parts from the inside.

PVC parts for the pressure chamber:

- 2 8" lengths of 2" pipe
- 1 15" length of 2" pipe
- 2 12" lengths of ½" pipe; one is the barrel, the other is the launch rod.
- 1 2" length of ½" pipe
- 1 3" length of ¾" pipe
- 1 2" tee (slip)
- 2 2" caps (slip)
- 1 ½" 90-degree elbow (slip and thread)
- 1 ½" 90-degree elbow (slip)
- 1 2"-to-1¾" coupling (slip)
- 1 1¾"-to-¾" bushing (slip)
- 2 ¾" male adapters (slip and thread)
- 1 ¾"-to-½" bushing (slip and thread)
- 2 ½"-to-½" male adapters (slip and thread)

You'll also need:

- Protective goggles
- 1 ¾" ball valve (threaded ends)
- PVC primer and cement; the cans include brushes.
- Tire valve with a long rubber-coated stem. We cut one off an old bicycle inner tube.

- Teflon tape
- Saw, or PVC shears
- Fine sandpaper
- Drill and ⁵⁄₁₆" bit ½
- Channel-lock pliers
- Duct tape

For the inclinometer you'll need:

- 1 1" wide piece of wood, approx. 20" long
- 1 1" wide piece of wood, approx 6" long
- 2 wood screws
- 1 long nail
- 1 short nail
- Drill with small bit
- Hammer
- Screwdriver
- 1 6" plastic 180-degree protractor (with a straight edge)
- 1 8" length of string
- 1 washer, or other weight

For the rockets you'll need:

- Several sheets of 8½x11" paper
- A 24" length of ½" PVC pipe, to use as a rocket construction rod
- Cellophane tape
- Ruler
- Protractor
- Scissors

To race your rockets you'll need:

- An open area, at least 1,000 sq. ft.
- Your rocket launcher
- Your inclinometer
- Bicycle pump with built-in pressure gauge
- Tape measure

Construct the pressure chamber

1. Using the ⁵⁄₁₆" drill bit, drill a hole in the center of one of the 2" caps. (The hole should be slightly smaller than the diameter of the tire valve stem. You might need to wiggle the bit to enlarge the hole.) Remove the valve stem's cap; from the inside of the PVC cap, jam the stem through the cap's hole. (Figure A) With duct tape, secure the stem in place—but don't cover the air hole (Figure B).

2. If you didn't have the PVC cut at the hardware store, use the saw or PVC shears now to cut the 8" and 15" lengths of 2" pipe, as well as the 12" lengths of ½" pipe.

3. Cement the two 8" lengths of 2" pipe to the ends of the tee, then cement the two caps onto the ends of these pipes (Figure C). Cement the 15" length of pipe to the tee's remaining opening. Onto the other end of the 15" length of pipe, cement the 2"-to-1¾" reducer coupling. Cement the 1¾"-to-¾" bushing to the coupling; then cement the 3" length of ¾" pipe to that bushing (Figures D and E).

> **CAUTION!** Use sandpaper to smooth all sawn PVC edges. When using PVC cement and primer, make sure that you have adequate ventilation. Prime all surfaces to be cemented, allow primer to dry, then coat the primed surfaces with cement. Using a twisting motion, quickly shove the parts together—then hold them firmly together for 30 seconds.

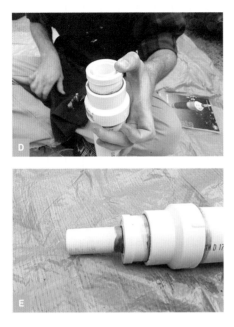

4. Wrap Teflon tape around the threads of one ¾" adapter (Figure F). Screw (don't cement) this adapter into the ball valve; use the channel-lock pliers to tighten (Figure G). Cement the other end of this adapter to the 3" length of ¾" pipe. Make sure that the valve's lever (in closed position) points straight up (Figure H).

5. Screw (don't cement) the second ¾" adapter into the other end of the ball valve. Cement the ¾"-to-½" bushing into this adapter (Figure I).

Construct the barrel

We'll build the barrel in a few sections, then join those sections together—because otherwise the launch rod might not point straight up into the sky when we're done.

1. Cement the slip-and-thread elbow onto the end of the rocket launcher's barrel (one of the two 12" lengths of ½" pipe) (Figure J). Screw (don't cement) the first ½"-to-½" adapter (slip and thread) into the threaded end of the elbow—not too tightly! You might want to adjust the angle later.

2. Cement one end of the 2" length of ½" pipe to the second slip elbow (Figure K). Then cement the other end of this pipe into the end of the first ½"-to-½" adapter from Step 1. You're going to want the open end of the second elbow to point straight up into the air.

3. Screw (don't cement) the second ½"-to-½" adapter into the bushing at the open end of the pressure chamber (Figure L). Finally, cement the rocket launcher's barrel to this second adapter (Figures M and N).

4. When you're ready to launch a rocket, insert the launch rod (the remaining 12" length of ½" pipe) into the open end of the elbow at the end of the barrel (Figure O).

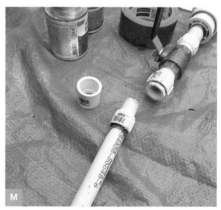

Build rockets

When you release air from the pressure chamber by opening the valve, the rocket at the end of the launch rod will fill with air and shoot off the rod; air expanding out of the rocket's open end will add thrust. Make your rocket streamlined by using small, straight fins.

Make your rockets out of standard copier paper. For better results, use heavier weight paper for the nose cone and fins

1. Roll a cylinder of paper around the construction rod, forming an 11"-long rocket body tube. Make sure the tube is slightly loose; it should slide freely along the construction rod. Tape the seam tightly and completely. Sliding the rocket body tube slightly off the rod, fold the top of the tube closed and tape it down tightly. Don't remove the rocket body tube from the rod yet.

2. To make a nose cone for your rocket, cut a half circle and curl its corners to form a cone shape. (The round edge forms the base of the cone; the straight edge folds in the middle to form the apex as the sides overlap.) Tape the seam, then place the cone over the closed end of the rocket body tube. Fit the cone to the outside dimension of the tube, trim off excess paper if necessary, and then tape the cone securely in place.

3. Cut rocket fins—we've included a diagram, but you are encouraged to experiment with other designs—and tape them to the lower end of the body tube.

4. Remove rocket from construction rod at the last minute before using, if possible.

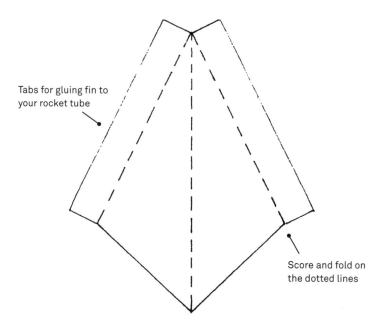

Tabs for gluing fin to your rocket tube

Score and fold on the dotted lines

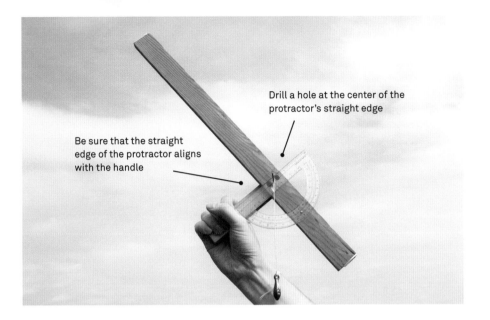

Drill a hole at the center of the protractor's straight edge

Be sure that the straight edge of the protractor aligns with the handle

Make an inclinometer

Foresters and land surveyors use inclinometers to measure the angle between the ground and the top of a tall object. If they know how far they are from the base of the object, then—using a bit of math—they can use the angle to deduce the object's height. We're going to build a simple inclinometer and use it as a launch altitude tracker.

1. Using the long piece of wood as the "barrel," and the short piece as the "handle," screw together a gun-shaped object.

2. Drill a small hole in the protractor, at the 90-degree point. If there isn't already a hole at the center of the protractor's straight edge (at the 3" point), then drill one there too.

3. Align the straight edge of the protractor with the inclinometer's handle; approximately 2 ½" of the protractor should extend above the barrel, and about 2 ½" below the barrel. Drive the

long nail into the inclinometer's barrel, through the protractor's 3" point. But don't drive the long nail all the way in; leave 1" sticking out, to serve as a fulcrum for the string and weight. As you can see from the example here, the nail fits perfectly between the two screws.

4. Making sure that the straight edge of the protractor remains aligned with the inclinometer's handle, drive the short nail into the inclinometer's barrel, through the hole you've drilled at the protractor's 90-degree point. The protractor should be firmly attached to the "gun," now.

5. Fasten the weight to one end of the string, then tie a small loop at the string's other end. Slip the loop over the protruding end of the long nail. Try aiming the inclinometer straight ahead, with your arm level to the ground; the string should cross the inclinometer's scale at the 180-degree point.

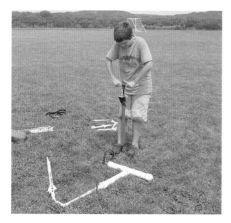

Race your rocket

1. Set the launcher on the ground. Make sure the valve is open, so there's no pressure in the chamber. Insert the launch rod into the rocket launcher's barrel, and aim the rod straight up.

2. Using the tape measure, establish a launch altitude tracking station 50' in front of the launcher.

3. During each player's turn, a second player must act as the rocket spotter. She will stand at the tracking station, holding the inclinometer. As the rocket rises into the air, the spotter will track its flight, aiming at the rocket along the inclinometer's "barrel." As she tilts the inclinometer, the weighted string will slide along the scale—away from the 180-degree point towards the 90-degree point.

4. Clear all spectators from the launch area.

5. Slide your rocket down the rod until it stops. Close the rocket launcher's valve. Using the bicycle pump, pump air (45 psi) into the pressure chamber.

6. Count down from 10 loudly, so that the rocket spotter and spectators are prepared. Then, bracing the pressure chamber with one hand, and making sure your head is not over the launch rod, move the valve lever quickly from "closed" to "open." Whooosh!

7. As soon as the rocket begins to tumble down, the spotter will freeze her arm in place, then use her thumb to press the string against the protractor—thus marking the angle between the ground and the rocket at its highest altitude. Relaxing her arm, the spotter can now announce the rocket's "angle score," which will be somewhere between 180 degrees and 90 degrees.

8. For each player in the game, repeat Steps 3 through 7. The player whose rocket had the lowest angle score—closest, that is, to 90 degrees—wins the game. Everyone else should build new rockets, experimenting with the shape and placement of the rocket fins.

We're very grateful to Lawry Hutcheson, for his rocket-launcher expertise.

ALKA-SELTZER BATTLE

The goal is to make your opponent's tablet fizz up and dissolve

Players: 2+

On a hot day, a squirt gun fight is fun—but it's not exactly a game. So here's an idea for gamifying this classic summer activity.

You'll need:
- Alka-Seltzer tablets
- String and scissors
- Drill with a sharp ¼" bit. Use with grownup supervision.
- Squirt guns

Try this:

1. Drill holes through the center of several Alka-Seltzer tablets, without breaking them.

2. Cut string into lengths appropriate for long necklaces.

3. Carefully thread a drilled tablet onto each piece of string, and knot the loose ends of string together.

4. Put on one necklace apiece.

5. Let the water fight begin! The goal is to make your opponent's tablet (or opponents' tablets) fizz up and dissolve before your own tablet does. You can run around squirting at each other, or you can make this game more of a target-shooting duel—where you begin back-to-back, take five steps away from one another, turn and start shooting without moving your feet.

BEST EVER
GLOBAL GAMES

Many of our favorite classic games—from chess to *Risk* to *Tetris*—hail from other parts of the world. Here are a few about which you might not have heard... until now. Enjoy!

Catch the Dragon's Tail: China
Players: 10+

To play this Chinese game, get a group of people to stand in a line—with each player placing their hands of the shoulders of the player in front of them. The first person in line is the dragon's head; the last person is the dragon's tail. The object of the game is for the head to catch the tail.

The first player in line maneuvers the line around so that he can tag the last player. All the players in the middle should wiggle, squirm, and do whatever else it takes to prevent the head from tagging the tail. (But don't break the line.) If the head catches the tail, then the last-in-line player becomes the dragon's new head. All other players move back one position.

Luta de Galo: Brazil
Players: 2+

This name of this popular Brazilian game—for which you'll need two bandannas, dishtowels, or other pieces of cloth—means "rooster battle."

Two players battle at a time. You each tuck a piece of cloth into the back of your belt or waistband, then cross your right arm across your chest. Then you each lift your left foot off the ground. (If your left foot touches the ground, or if you uncross your right arm, you lose automatically.) Now hop around trying to snatch your opponent's "tail" with your left hand!

For a chaotically good time, distribute cloth tails to everyone—and have everyone battle at once.

If your left foot touches the ground, then you lose

Mancala: East Africa

Players: 2

Most likely invented long ago in East Africa, the goal of this count-and-capture game is to end up with more stones in your *kahala* (home cup) than your opponent has in hers.

You can buy a mancala board, but why not make one of your own? Cut the lid off an egg carton, and place it horizontally between yourself and your opponent—so you're each facing a row of six cups. Divide 48 dried beans evenly between the carton's twelve cups. Each player places their *kahala* (use a jar, mug, or bowl) at the end of the board to their right.

On your turn, scoop all the beans from any one of the six cups on your side of the board. Moving counter-clockwise from the now-empty cup, drop one bean into each cup until you run out of beans—at which point it's your opponent's turn. If you reach your own *kahala* along the way, drop a bean into it. (If the last bean you drop goes into your *kahala*, you get an extra turn!) However, if you reach your opponent's *kahala*, skip it.

If the last bean you drop goes into an *empty* cup on your side of the board, you capture not only that bean but any beans in the cup directly opposite—i.e., on your opponent's side of the board. All captured beans go into your *kahala*.

When all six cups on one side of the board are empty, the game ends. The player who still has beans on her side of the board adds those beans to her *kahala*. Now count 'em up.

Kabaddi: South Asia

Players: 14

In order to play this wrestling sport from South Asia, you'll need two teams—who begin by standing on opposite sides of a grassy field divided in half.

Each team takes a turn sending a "raider" across the field. For each member of the opposing team that the raider tags—while repeatedly chanting the word "Kabaddi" *without ever taking a breath*, then running back to his team's side of the field *while still chanting*—he scores one point for his team. If a raider runs out of breath, or fails to tag anyone, he's out of the game.

There are other rules, but playing tag while chanting is enough of a challenge to get you started.

Pass the Parcel: United Kingdom

Players: 4+

This British party game is fun to make *and* play. You'll need a small prize, a small box, plenty of paper (tissue paper or newspaper works best, but you can use any kind), tape, a source of music, and a referee who can start and stop the music.

Put the prize into the box. Wrap the box like a gift, and tape the wrapping together. Then wrap it again. And again, and again, until you have at least 10 layers of wrapping around the box.

Have all players sit in a circle. When the music starts, pass the present around the circle; when the music stops, the person holding the present unwraps a layer. Repeat until the present is completely unwrapped. The person who unwraps the last layer wins the prize.

GOOGLE EARTH
CHALLENGES

Google Earth is a 3-D virtual globe. It provides so much local detail that a few years ago, an adopted man used it to locate his hometown in India... which he hadn't seen since he was five! But most people simply use it as a way to explore the planet from their own home.

There are many exploration games that you can play using Google Earth and Google Maps—the best-known of which is Google Earth's built-in Flight Simulator mode. Here are a few favorites.

Monster Milktruck
goo.gl/6KzmFe
Enter your own address—or choose a location anywhere in the world—and drive a milk truck through the streets like a maniac. Set a challenge, such as navigating through San Francisco to the Golden Gate Bridge. Or try to get from the center of your own city or town back to your house. If you stop for too long, the truck will complain: "I'm sitting here getting sour."

GeoGuessr
geoguessr.com
This game drops you into a random Google Street View locale and challenges you to figure out where you are now. Take in every little clue: Are there trees—and if so, what species? What color is the soil? If there are road signs or billboards, do you recognize the language? You can play Geoguessr against yourself, or against players around the world.

Ships
planetinaction.com/ships15
A Google Earth-based game that lets you choose a huge ocean-going vessel (barges, cruise ships, even container ships), one of four viewing angles, and your port of call. As you steer toward your destination, don't forget to sound the foghorn!

SMARTPHONE
SCAVENGER HUNT

Include hard-to-find items like "a video of birds in flight"

Players: 2+

Tech up the classic outdoor locating game. And clean up your neighborhood while you're at it.

You'll need:

- A cameraphone per team
- A small bag (to pick up trash)
- **Optional:** Pencil and paper for each team

Try this:

1. Appoint a referee.

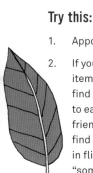

2. If you are the referee, make a list of items that players might be able to find and photograph nearby. In addition to easy ones like "a red leaf" or "a friendly neighbor," include harder-to-find items such as "a video of birds in flight." Toss in categories like "something that begins with the letter B." Make each team photograph or video one of its members doing something theatrical, like "pretend you're a troll under a bridge."

   Note: Each list should include "trash found on the street"; instead of taking a photo, players collect the trash and bring it back.

3. Divide into teams. Members of each team write down the things to search for, using the smartphone's notes function, say, or else pencil and paper.

4. Set the timers on your phones to the agreed-upon time.

5. Start hunting! When you find an item from your list, photograph or video it, depending on the instructions.

6. Return to the referee before time runs out. The team with the most items from the list photographed wins. In the case of a tie, the team with the most garbage collected wins.

➡ HACKS

- Do a scavenger hunt in a forest, or a shopping mall, or downtown.
- Make the hunt about a specific theme—fashion, cars, mushrooms.
- Use bicycles and/or public transportation, so you can roam farther.

Illustrations by Heather Kasunick

QUEENING

AN EXCERPT FROM

THROUGH THE LOOKING-GLASS

by Lewis Carroll

Through the Looking-Glass, an 1871 sequel to *Alice in Wonderland* by Lewis Carroll, uses a game of chess played on a giant chessboard (with fields for squares) as its theme. Alice begins the story as a pawn; however, if she can move all the way to the board's eighth row, she will become a queen—this is a reference to chess's Rule of Promotion, or "Queening."

For some minutes Alice stood without speaking, looking out in all directions over the country—and a most curious country it was. There were a number of tiny little brooks running straight across it from side to side, and the ground between was divided up into squares by a number of little green hedges, that reached from brook to brook.

"I declare it's marked out just like a large chessboard!" Alice said at last. "There ought to be some men moving about somewhere—and so there are!" she added in a tone of delight, and her heart began to beat quick with excitement as she went on. "It's a great huge game of chess that's being played—all over the world—if this *is* a world at all, you know. Oh, what fun it is! How I *wish* I was one of them! I wouldn't mind being a Pawn, if only I might join—though of course I should *like* to be a Queen, best."

She glanced rather shyly at the real Queen as she said this, but her companion only smiled pleasantly, and said, "That's easily managed. You can be the White Queen's Pawn, if you like, as Lily's too young to play; and you're in the Second Square to begin with: when you get to the Eighth Square you'll be a Queen —" Just at this moment, somehow or other, they began to run.

"While you're refreshing yourself," said the Queen, "I'll just take the measurements." And she took a ribbon out of her pocket, marked in inches, and began measuring the ground, and sticking little pegs in here and there.

"At the end of two yards," she said, putting in a peg to mark the distance, "I shall give you your directions […] At the end of *three* yards I shall repeat them—for fear of your forgetting them. At the end of *four*, I shall say good-bye. And at the end of *five*, I shall go!"

She had got all the pegs put in by this time, and Alice looked on with great interest as she returned to the tree, and then began slowly walking down the row.

At the two-yard peg she faced round, and said, "A pawn goes two squares in its first move, you know. So you'll go *very* quickly through the Third Square—by railway, I should think—and you'll find yourself in the Fourth Square in no time. Well, *that* square belongs to Tweedledum and Tweedledee—the Fifth is mostly water—the Sixth belongs to Humpty Dumpty—But you make no remark?"

"I—I didn't know I had to make one—just then," Alice faltered out.

"You *should* have said," the Queen went on in a tone of grave reproof, "'It's extremely kind of you to tell me all this'—however, we'll suppose it said—the Seventh Square is all forest—however, one of the Knights will show you the way—and in the Eighth Square we shall be Queens together, and it's all feasting and fun!" Alice got up and curtseyed, and sat down again.

At the next peg the Queen turned again, and this time she said, "Speak in French when you can't think of the English for a thing—turn out your toes as you walk—and remember who you are!" She did not wait for Alice to curtsey this time, but walked on quickly to the next peg, where she turned for a moment to say "good-bye," and then hurried on to the last.

How it happened, Alice never knew, but exactly as she came to the last peg, she was gone. Whether she vanished into the air, or whether she ran quickly into the wood ("and she *can* run very fast!" thought Alice), there was no way of guessing, but she was gone, and Alice began to remember that she was a Pawn, and that it would soon be time for her to move.

PLAY
FOURSQUARE
(THE APP)

Check in from
wherever you are

The social city-guide app *Foursquare*
is a fun way to explore your neighborhood, town, or city with the help
of a smartphone, a phone with a web
browser, or via text messaging.

Foursquare's users around the world mostly use it to broadcast their current location
to friends. But it's also a game that rewards
you for discovering new places; and you
can compete with others. It's these aspects
of *Foursquare*—the ones that encourage
users to get to know their town or city
better—that you and your grownup might
enjoy together.

Checking in
When you tell *Foursquare* where you are,
that's called "checking in." The *Foursquare*
apps for the iPhone, Blackberry, and
Android use GPS to show you a list of
nearby locations. You can check in from
parks, museums, houses, stores, librar-
ies… anywhere. If *Foursquare* doesn't
have the place you're looking for, you can
add it to the app's listings.

Don't worry, *Foursquare* doesn't know
where you are unless you check in to tell
the app your location; also, if you prefer,
you can check in without broadcasting
your location to friends.

Learn about your town
Whenever you check in, *Foursquare* will
recommend places to go and things to
do nearby. If your friends use *Foursquare*,
you'll learn more about their favorite
spots and the new places they discover
(and vice versa).

Illustrations by Mister Reusch

You the mayor

Foursquare is sort of like a videogame, but instead of playing the game indoors in front of a TV, you're visiting unfamiliar places around your own hometown.

Every *Foursquare* check-in earns you points. Find a new place in your neighborhood? +5 points. Dragging friends along with you? +1. And so forth. As you start checking in to more and more new places, you'll unlock badges.

If you've been to a place more often than anyone else, you'll become the "mayor" of that place on *Foursquare*—which can mean discounts and freebies. Or just bragging rights.

> **IMPORTANT!** *Foursquare* users must be 13 to subscribe, and the online interaction isn't moderated. So kids under 13 can and should only use this app with their grownup.

Compete against your friends to discover new places

FOURSQUARE BADGES

Newbie
Awarded for your first check-in.

Adventurer
Check in to 10 different venues.

Explorer
Check in to 25 different venues.

Superstar
Check in to 50 different venues.

Local
Check in at the same place three times in a week.

Don't Stop Believin'
Check in to three venues tagged "karaoke."

Zoetrope
Have 10 movie theater check-ins.

Pizzaiolo
Check in to 20 different pizza places.

THE SECRET HISTORY of MMOGs

1. *MASSIVELY MULTIPLAYER ONLINE GAMES ARE MASSIVELY POPULAR — A DOZEN NEW ONES APPEAR EACH YEAR. BUT WHEN YOUR GROWN-UPS WERE KIDS, MMOGS DIDN'T EXIST! SO WHERE DID THEY COME FROM?

3. AND LARPING — A RPG IN WHICH YOU PHYSICALLY ACT OUT YOUR CHARACTER, TRANSFORMING THE REAL WORLD INTO A GAMESPACE — REALLY TOOK OFF IN THE 1970s.

1970s BEWARE!

LIGHTNING BOLT!

2. BEFORE VIDEOGAME + COMPUTER RPGS, THERE WAS DUNGEONS + DRAGONS, A TABLETOP ROLE-PLAYING GAME PUBLISHED IN 1974. INVENTORS DAVE ARNESON + GARY GYGAX GAVE US KEY GAME MECHANICS LIKE AVATARS, CHARACTER SKILLS REPRESENTED BY "STATS", AND "LEVELING UP".

15. THANKS TO THE RISE OF WEARABLE TECH — EYEGLASSES, WRISTLETS, EVEN CLOTHES THAT MAKE CONSTANT INTERACTION BETWEEN YOU AND YOUR COMPUTER POSSIBLE — MMOGs ARE ABOUT TO GET A LOT MORE INTERESTING. THE REAL WORLD MIGHT BECOME THE LATEST AND GREATEST GAME SPACE... WHICH, IF YOU THINK ABOUT IT, IS PRETTY MUCH WHERE OUR QUEST TO DISCOVER THE ORIGINS OF MMOGs BEGAN!

12. AT THE TURN OF THE 21ST CENTURY THE 'SIXTH GENERATION' ERA OF HOME GAMING BEGAN. PLATFORMS LIKE THE PS3, GAMECUBE, AND XBOX MADE IT POSSIBLE TO PLAY MMOGs NOT ONLY ON YOUR COMPUTER, BUT ON YOUR VIDEOGAME SYSTEM, TOO. MICROSOFT'S XBOX LIVE MULTIPLAYER SERVICE WAS FIRST LAUNCHED IN 2002.

2000

THE 2010's

13. WORLD OF WARCRAFT, WHICH GOT ITS START AS A REAL-TIME STRATEGY COMPUTER GAME IN THE 1990's WAS RELAUNCHED IN 2004 AS A MMOG.

TODAY, ITS THE MOST POPULAR GAME OF ITS KIND, WITH OVER 8 MILLION MONTHLY SUBSCRIBERS.

14. ANOTHER DEVELOPMENT OF THE 2000s: MOBILE MMOGs, LIKE 2001's *SAMURAI ROMANESQUE*. GAMES IN WHICH A PLAYER COULD GO ANYWHERE COULD NOW BE PLAYED ANYWHERE.

4. SHORTLY AFTER D+D APPEARED, THE TEXT BASED COMPUTER GAME **ADVENTURE** GAVE US THE FIRST DIGITAL GAMESPACE A PLAYER COULD EXPLORE FREELY — INSTEAD OF PROCEEDING IN A LINEAR PATTERN.

5. (ADVENTURE CREATOR WILL CROWTHER WAS AN AVID EXPLORER OF KENTUCKY'S MAMMOTH CAVE SYSTEM)

6. ADVENTURE WAS QUICKLY FOLLOWED BY THE EVEN-MORE SOPHISTICATED GAME, **ZORK**.

7. IN ADDITION TO RPGS AND NEW GAMESPACES, THE 1970s SAW THE ADVENT OF THE INTERNET. THANKS TO THIS GLOBAL COMPUTER NETWORK, ORIGINALLY DEVELOPED FOR MILITARY AND SCIENTIFIC PURPOSES, GAMERS WOULD EVENTUALLY BE ABLE TO PLAY TOGETHER, ON THE INTERNET.

1980s

8. USING THE PROGRAMMING LANGUAGE 'C', AROUND 1980 TWO COLLEGE STUDENTS PROGRAMMED **ROGUE**, ONE OF THE FIRST-EVER GRAPHICS-BASED COMPUTER ADVENTURE GAMES. ALL ASPECTS OF THIS DUNGEON-CRAWLING GAME, INCLUDING THE AVATAR ITSELF, WERE DRAWN USING NUMBERS AND LETTERS.

9. ONE OF THE FIRST GRAPHICAL MULTIPLAYER ONLINE GAMES WAS A WORLD WAR II AIR COMBAT SIMULATOR INTRODUCED IN 1987. AIR WARRIOR DEMONSTRATED THAT — FINALLY! — COMPUTER GRAPHICS WERE GOOD ENOUGH, AND NETWORKS FAST ENOUGH, FOR MMOGS.

11. DURING THE 1990s, A CASCADE OF MMOGS THAT ARE NOW LEGENDARY APPEARED IN RAPID SUCCESSION: MERIDIAN 95 IN 1995, THE REALM ONLINE IN '96, ULTIMA ONLINE IN '97, NEXUS IN '98, AND EVERQUEST IN '99.

AOL 1990s

10. ONCE THE PUBLISHER OF AIR WARRIOR PARTNERED WITH THE HUGELY POPULAR ONLINE SERVICE PROVIDER **AOL** TO PRODUCE THE GAME **NEVERWINTER NIGHTS** (WHICH ALLOWED 50 PEOPLE TO PLAY SIMULTANEOUSLY) IN 1991 THE RACE WAS ON!

GEO-GAMES

Geodashing can be played by individuals or teams

The goal is to reach a dashpoint quickly

Players: 1+

In our book *Unbored*, we encouraged readers to try geocaching, a fun and free GPS-based treasure-hunting game. Geocachers around the world have hidden over a million caches (containers, often filled with prizes), then uploaded their latitude and longitude so you can locate them.

GPS users have also dreamed up the following adventuresome games. You can download a geocaching app and try out these games today—right in your own neighborhood. Note that the organizers of these games encourage respect for private property and the environment.

You'll need:
- A GPS device, or a smartphone with GPS

Geodashing
Geodashing is a game whose players use GPS devices to reach as many "dash-points" (locations selected randomly, by a computer program; they might be in suburban neighborhoods, in city squares, or out in the woods) as possible within a given period of time. Geodashing players can participate as individuals or as teams of up to five players; the competition is friendly and teamwork helps. Note that there is nothing to find once you reach the dashpoint; the goal is simply to get there—if you can.

From your computer at home, use the tools at Geodashing.GPSgames.org to find the current game's dashpoints near you. Using your GPS unit or geocaching app, visit the dashpoint—you must get within 100 meters of it. Whoever gets there first, scores 3 points in the game; the second player or group scores 2 points; all other players score 1 point… so you might as well try reaching it, even if you're not the first! You'll document your achievement by uploading a descriptive report to the website, along with (optional) a scenic photo of the spot.

Waymarking

Waymarking is a hide-and-seek game that's more about seeking than hiding. People who come across interesting places or things upload photos of them, along with longitude and latitude coordinates. So far, there are over a quarter-million such "waymarks," ranging from turtle crossings, quonset huts, blacksmith shops, lighthouses, tattoo parlors, and pick-your-own farms to graffiti, carousels, gargoyles, model railroads, outdoor chess games, vintage advertisements, ghost towns, mountain summits, fossils, home-made mailboxes, haunted houses, and water wheels. The object of the game is to find the waymark—using your GPS unit or geocaching app—and log it, at the website Waymarking.com.

Seek out benchmarks by entering your zip code at geocaching.com/mark

Benchmark Hunting

Have you ever noticed—while hiking on top of a mountain, say, or strolling through a village square—a small bronze disc, set into concrete or rock, that reads "U.S. Coast & Geodetic Survey Bench-mark," or "National Oceanic Survey Benchmark," or perhaps "U.S. Geological Survey Benchmark"? Each of these bench-marks is a location used by surveyors and cartographers to confirm either the precise elevation (above sea level) of that location, or else the precise latitude and longitude of that elevation. Or both.

The latitude and longitude of many of these markers are included in the National Spatial Reference System, a database maintained by the National Geodetic Survey (NGS), a US federal agency whose data is used, to mention just one crucial example, by the Federal Emergency Management Agency in order to determine flood zones. But NGS data is also used by geocachers! By entering your postal code at geocaching.com/mark, you can find information about benchmarks in your immediate area. Once you've chosen one, seek it out using your GPS unit or geocaching app, and/or written directions provided by the NGS.

Confluence Hunting

On a map, the points where lines of longitude and latitude cross are called "degree confluence points." The over 64,000 real-world places where these imaginary lines intersect—that's 360 degrees of longitude multiplied by 180 degrees of latitude—have sparked the imagination of confluence hunters around the world. Volunteers with the Degree Confluence Project are making an effort to visit each degree confluence point on the planet (approximately 16,000 of them are on land, the rest are on water) and document it with photos. You can, too!

Visit the Degree Confluence Project's website (Confluence.org) to get started, or just unfold a fairly detailed map of your county or state and figure out which confluence points are nearby. You're probably no more than 50 miles away from one right now! Whether you and your grownup are getting there by car, bicycle, or on foot, you'll want to use your GPS unit or geocaching app. When you get to the confluence point, snap a photo. Back home, you can upload it to Confluence. org… and enjoy exploring the website's huge collection of photos.

CONFLUENCE CANNONBALL!

MINDGAME

HOW MANY?

The natural tendency of the human brain is to take the fuzzy flux of data that pours in through the eyes and ears, and divide it up into manageable chunks. If we didn't do that, we'd just end up lying in a baffled haze. And this is where numbers came from. You might assume they were invented by a secret society of schoolteachers for the purposes of tormenting the brains of poor, innocent children. It's a reasonable assumption, but an incorrect one.

Can you tell what's being counted in each of the six phrases below? (Here's an example to help you. The phrase "60 S in a M" would expand to "60 seconds in a minute.")

1. 366 D in a LY
2. 26 L in the A
3. 12 S of the Z
4. 100 C in a D
5. 13 C in a S
6. 16 O in a P

MAKE & BREAK A PIÑATA

Players: The more the merrier

Although they are often associated with Mexico, paper piñatas originated in China in the 1500s and then eventually made their way to Italy, where clay pots were filled with goodies and then held up high so they could be smashed with sticks.

While you can buy a piñata almost anywhere, it's more fun to make one yourself.

You'll need:
- 2 cups flour
- 2 cups water
- 1 tablespoon salt
- Bowl
- Lots of newspaper
- Scissors
- Balloons
- Tissue paper
- Paper cupcake cups
- White glue
- Twine or string
- Box cutter; use with grownup supervision
- Candy or other small prizes
- **Optional:** ribbons, glitter, other doodads

IMPORTANT! Piñatas take a lot of time to make. Start this activity at least three days before your party.

Try this:

1. Make the paste by mixing the flour, water, and salt together in a bowl. Add additional water if the mixture isn't thin enough to spread easily.

Illustrations by Mister Reusch

2. Cut up lots of 2"x8"-wide strips of newspaper.

3. Blow up a balloon and tie it. This is your basic form for the piñata. You can attach bunched-up newspaper or paper cups or cones to create shapes.

4. Dip strips of newspaper into the paste and then place them on the balloon, making a criss-cross pattern. You can also just place the strips on the balloon and use your hands to rub the paste all over them, taking care to leave a little bit of space around the balloon knot. Make 3 or 4 layers. Note: It can take an entire night for the newspaper to dry. It's quicker if you leave the piñata outside.

5. When the newspaper is dry, take a pin or needle and poke a hole in the balloon, which should be peeking out from the top of the piñata. Pull the now deflated balloon out through the top hole where the balloon knot used to be.

6. Poke two holes into opposing ends of the top of the piñata, and string 10" of strong twine or string through them to create a loop for hanging.

7. Put candy or other prizes in the piñata through the hole where the balloon knot used to be (you and your grownup might need to use a box cutter to make it a bit wider.

8. Using the newspaper strips and paste, paper over the hole. Let dry.

9. Start decorating! Traditional piñatas use strips of colored tissue paper that are folded and then cut with tiny slits to make a fringe. We think it's easier to paste paper cupcake cups all over it. But you don't have to stop there: Ribbons, glitter, sequins, loops of yarn—make it happen.

10. Time to play! In addition to your piñata, you'll need a blindfold, some kind of stick (a broomstick handle works best), and rope. Hang the piñata so that it's high enough that players have to reach up to hit it. It's best if you hang it over a branch or beam so that a grownup can raise, lower or swing it to make the game more challenging. On your turn, put on a blindfold and take three swings at the piñata. When it finally breaks, everyone rushes to get as many prizes as they can.

HIDE-AND-SEEK
HACKS

Players 4+

Illustrations by Heather Kasunick

These Hide-and-Seek variants are popular getting-to-know-you games at summer camps… because whoever is "It" must learn everyone's name. But they can also be played in urban parks, vacant lots, and even on the street in front of your house.

DOTS

You'll need:
- A large playing area, with plenty of places to hide.

Try this:

1. Agree on the course's "checkpoints"— specific objects, all of which can be viewed from the course's final checkpoint. The checkpoints should be neither too far apart from one another,

nor too close. At the same time, decide the order in which these checkpoints must be touched; usually, the course will form a rough circle.

2. Gather at the final checkpoint. Choose one person to be the Hunter; the other players are Hiders. The Hunter announces a number, and also how quickly (fast, medium, slow) he'll be counting. For example: "Five, slow," means the Hunter will count slowly from 1 to 5.

3. The Hunter closes his eyes and counts, loudly and clearly, while the Hiders run the course, touching each checkpoint in order. Once the Hunter counts to the final number, he opens his eyes; if he spots any Hiders, he yells their names,

and those players must return to the start. If you're a Hider, a few seconds before the Hunter finishes counting, you should dive into hiding!

4. The Hunter announces a new number (and how quickly he'll count), closes his eyes, and counts. The Hiders who'd been hiding emerge and continue running the course. The Hiders who were spotted start the course over. When a Hider makes it around the entire course, she tags the Hunter— then waits for the others to finish.

5. Once every Hider has made it around the entire course, the game ends.

The Fox tries to freeze every Rabbit

The Rabbits try to reach Home Base

Home base

FOX IN THE FIELD

You'll need:
- A large playing area, with plenty of places to hide.

Try this:

1. Choose an object (a tree, or telephone pole, usually) to be Home Base.

2. Choose one player to be the Fox; the other players are Rabbits. Introduce yourselves, so that the Fox knows everyone's name.

3. Standing at Home Base, the Fox closes her eyes and counts loudly to 60. The Rabbits scatter and hide. The Fox opens her eyes and starts running around the field, searching for hidden Rabbits. Meanwhile, the Rabbits emerge from hiding and scamper for Home Base.

4. Whenever the Fox spots a Rabbit, she yells, "One-two-three, I see [name of player]." That Rabbit is now frozen until another Rabbit runs up and un-freezes him by tagging him.

5. When all the Rabbits reach Home Base, or if the Fox freezes every Rabbit, the game ends.

MINDGAME

REASONING

You probably know Zeus. He was the big guy with a beard who had the thankless job of keeping all the other gods in line on Mount Olympus. Rumor has it that he would often get fed up of all the bickering and name-calling and would retreat to a quiet cave on some lesser-known Mediterranean island for a bit of peace and quiet. During these meditative time-outs, he would try to distract himself from all the divine melodrama by setting himself mental challenges.

On this particular day, sick as he was of all the verbal poop-flinging, he teleported to his godcave and applied his superhuman brain to the task of listing his fellow male Olympians (Apollo, Ares, Hephaestus, Hermes and Poseidon) in increasing order of their height. "What's so difficult about that?" you might ask. But Zeus is getting on a bit now and his memory isn't what it used to be. When his godly ungovernables aren't standing in front of him, all he can he remember about their heights is the following:

- Poseidon is taller than Hephaestus.
- Ares is taller than Hermes but shorter than Apollo.
- Hermes is taller than Hephaestus.
- Apollo is shorter than Poseidon.

After scratching his hairy chin and frowning for a while, he was eventually able to deduce the correct order of all five gods. Can you do the same?

PLAY A ROLE!

Q&A with Lizzie Stark

Kids enjoy role-playing games where the participants physically act out their characters. Grownups who enjoy this sort of thing call it live action role playing, or "larp."

Using real-world settings and objects to symbolize settings and objects from their game, larpers interact with each other in character—competing and cooperating to reach a goal. Sometimes the rules of their larping are decided by a gamemaster.

In *Leaving Mundania: Inside the Transformative World of Live Action Role-Playing Games*, writer Lizzie Stark explains what it's all about. Here's what she told us.

UNBORED: **What is the single biggest thing non-larpers misunderstand about larp?**

STARK: Larp has the rap of being "weird." But dressing up to be a character in a story isn't any weirder than wearing a football jersey and painting your face to cheer on your favorite sports team. Larp is playing make-believe, only instead of playing cops-and-robbers, say, you play cops-and-robbers with rules about who shoots first.

UNBORED: **Is larp a new kind of game?**

STARK: No. There is a long tradition of dressing up in costume and making a spectacle. Queen Elizabeth I used to go to parties where figures who were dressed up like they were from ancient myths jumped out of the shrubs and got her to play along with them.

UNBORED: **Do you have any tips for creating a great larp character?**

STARK: It's important to figure out what you like. If you like talking and solving problems by talking, then it might make sense to make a character who talks a lot. If you like being sneaky, then maybe it makes sense to create a character who is a spy. A lot of people make characters who are loners—that's a bad idea, because larping is about interacting with other people. It's also wise to avoid having your

Photo by J.R. Blackwell

character's story entirely figured out. If you have already discovered everything there is to know about your character, there's not much left to play.

UNBORED: Is it normal to feel self-conscious when you start larping?

STARK: Absolutely. The first thirty minutes of a game can be particularly awkward—while people are figuring out how the conversations are supposed to go. But if you are larping with experienced gamers, they are extremely friendly and help you get into your character. Gamemasters sometimes run a workshop at the start of the game where people can meet each other and develop their characters. You can practice walking like your character, for example, or think about phrases your character uses.

UNBORED: Any advice for kids who might want to be a larp's gamemaster?

STARK: There isn't always a gamemaster. But when there is, it's a collaboration between you and your players—and you are only as good as the experience you are giving to your players. A really bossy game master isn't great because people don't like to be bossed around. You are all in the story together.

UNBORED: What's the best thing about larping?

STARK: The people! I love getting together with others and making a story together. It always surprises me how much the other players improve the story.

It's up to the players to improve the story

Get into your character!

LARPING &
ARGS

BRAINS...

Illustrations by Mister Reusch

How to larp

Live-action roleplaying (larping) is a game where players don't sit at a table with papers and dice; instead, they get into character—and often into costume—and transport themselves to an imaginary world. How? By acting out the game's plot together, they imaginatively escape the real world and inhabit a fantastic play space. A house, for example, can become a castle—its basement a dungeon, its front porch a steep battlement.

Most people associate larping with fantasy role-playing games like *Dungeons & Dragons*, because the first larp that most people heard of was "Hobbit Wars." In this version of the game, which started in the 1970s, teams of players—dressed in costumes, and using foam-covered weapons to battle—compete in a Capture the Flag-style game. To play a game like "Hobbit Wars," you'll need a large open space, and some agreed-upon rules.

If you're not interested in hobbits and elves, you can use science fiction as the context for your game—perhaps you're explorers on a planet inhabited by strange beings who aren't thrilled to meet you? Perhaps you're under attack from zombies—or perhaps you *are* zombies? You can larp about Harry Potter, The Hunger Games, superheroes, you name it. When kids playing football or baseball pretend they're professionals… that's larping, too.

Although your grownups might need to be persuaded to gallivant through the neighborhood dressed as an elf, be patient with them! The important thing is training them to be imaginative and spontaneous. The rest will come eventually.

How to play an ARG

An alternate-reality game (ARG) is a group activity in which you usually play yourself, not an imaginary role or character. The goal of an ARG is not to escape the everyday world, but instead to transform the everyday world into a game space. In other words, you play an ARG in your real life; in the process, you discover "gameful" ways of interacting with the real world.

How does an ARG work? An ARG designer will dream up a game scenario—for example, one in which the world has run out of fuel. She then gathers players together for a game in which everyone behaves as though the world has actually run out of fuel for anywhere between an hour and a day. How do you feed yourself? How do you travel? What do you do for light and heat when the sun goes down? These are the questions and scenarios that get answered during the game.

An ARG designer can run the game via text messages

TiNAGMom 4:27PM
The fuel crisis has led to the emergence of a zombie army!

Transportation during a fuel crisis—your new reality

An ARG designer can also run the game via social media and text messages, sending challenges to players, who can keep the game going for days, weeks, sometimes even months.

Players in an ARG do whatever they would do if they found their reality altered in whatever way the ARG's designer has chosen to alter reality. There is only one rule of this sort of game: "This is not a game" (TINAG). Which is to say, the way to play the game is to treat it as your new reality. Use the tools you use in everyday life to navigate this tweaked new world!

There are hundreds of ARGs going on all the time; one place to find them is at the website ARGNet (argn.com). But you—and your grownup—can make up your own ARG. Just dream up an odd twist on the world in which you live, and invite everyone you know to participate.

Highlighted words in the puzzles throughout this book tell a strange tale

MINDGAME

THE FINAL PUZZLE

This is the tenth and final puzzle in the book. You may not have paid much attention to them up until now, but each of these previous teasers contains a word highlighted in white. When these words are combined and assembled in the correct order, they will reveal a troubling portent of an alternate (perhaps future?) universe.

MINDGAMES ANSWER KEY

The Only…: States 1. CONNECTICUT 2. ARIZONA 3. ALABAMA 4. DELAWARE 5. IOWA 6. MISSISSIPPI

The Only…: MLB Teams 1. TWINS 2. ORIOLES 3. NATIONALS 4. BRAVES 5. ASTROS 6. PHILLIES

Hidden Words: Board Games 1. MONOPOLY 2. SCRABBLE 3. CHESS 4. RISK 5. SORRY 6. CARCASSONNE

Hidden Words: Zoo Animals 1. GORILLA 2. HYENA 3. BEAR 4. LION 5. ZEBRA 6. LEOPARD

Anagrams: Harry Potter Characters 1. ALBUS DUMBLEDORE 2. HERMIONE GRANGER 3. RUBEUS HAGRID 4. SEVERUS SNAPE 5. NEVILLE LONGBOTTOM 6. MINERVA MCGONAGALL

What's Next? 1. D (December) 2. T (Ten) 3. Y (Years) 4. N (Neptune) 5. ROTJ (Return of the Jedi) 6. HPATDH (*Harry Potter and the Deathly Hallows*)

Anagrams: Lord of the Rings Characters 1. BILBO BAGGINS 2. PEREGRINE TOOK 3. FRODO BAGGINS 4. SAMWISE GAMGEE 5. MERIADOC BRANDYBUCK 6. LEGOLAS GREENLEAF

How Many? 1. DAYS, LEAP YEAR 2. LETTERS, ALPHABET 3. SIGNS, ZODIAC 4. CENTS, DOLLAR 5. CARDS, SUIT 6. OUNCES, POUND

Reasoning Poseidon, Apollo, Ares, Hermes, Hephaestus

The Final Puzzle Here's a hint: Look at the picture on this page.

RESOURCES

Pwnage

American Boy's Book of Sports and Games, The: A Practical Guide to Indoor and Outdoor Amusements (1864, 2000), by Barry Leonard. Classic games from yesteryear—including playground games (e.g., Baste the Bear, Prisoner's Base, King Senio) and parlor games (One Old Ox Opening Oysters, The Emperor of Morocco, Prussian Exercise). It's not just for boys.

American Girl's Handy Book, The: How To Amuse Yourself and Others (1887, 2009), by Lina Beard and Adelia Beard. More old-school games, organized according to the calendar. There are games for Easter, Fourth of July, Halloween, Thanksgiving, Christmas—there's even a Fern-Leaf Game appropriate for Midsummer's Eve. Not just for girls.

Big Book of Boy Stuff, The (2004), by Bart King. Among many other activities, this book—which features a reversible cover, so it can be disguised as a textbook—includes high-energy games such as Educated Elwood (Simple Simon in reverse), Liars' Dice, Grape Races, El Globo, Flying Shoes, Water Balloon Jousting, and Rounders. Not just for boys.

Book of Card Games, The (2013), by Nikki Katz. Not only does Katz teach you how to play six versions of Rummy, but she brings back classics, family favorites, and forgotten games like Canasta, Spoons, and even Oh Hell!, plus solitaire games like Clock, Free Cell, and Klondike.

Cokesbury Game Book, The (1939, 1960), by Arthur M. Depew. A few hundred old-fashioned active games (e.g., Defend the Fort, Weathercocks, The Accused), quiet games (Conundrum Baseball, Forfeits, Snapping Proverbs), writing games (Dictionary Girls, Transpositions, Literary Sandwiches), outdoor games (Snake and Crab Race, Peg), and more.

Games Bible, The (2010), by Leigh Anderson. The author has collected 300 games, including icebreakers (e.g., Name Boggle, Psychological Scavenger Hunt), guessing games (Breakfast Combo, Monster Movie Charades), right-brain games (Blindfolded Pictionary, Self-Portrait), games of general cleverness (Guggenheim, Iron Chef Potluck), and outdoor games (Jesse James, Urban Bingo). Plus 18 games—like Ministry of Silence and iPod Dance Charades—created by Jane McGonigal and other talented game designers.

Hopscotch, Hangman, Hot Potato, and Ha Ha Ha (1990), by Jack Maguire. Rules to more than 250 indoor, outdoor, water, party, and travel games. We particularly like the "Games to Play on Pavement, Steps, and Stoops" chapter, which includes the rules to classics like Battleball, German, London, O'Leary, Pottsie, Sidewalk Golf, Skully, and Stoopball.

Hoyle's Rules of Games (1742, 2001), by Albert H. Morehead, Geoffrey Mott-Smith, and Philip D. Morehead. Edmond Hoyle's 18th-century book on games has been updated to include rules, strategies, and odds for over 250 games—from *Scrabble* to Backgammon, to card games like Slapjack and solitaire games like Pyramid and Pounce.

Pocket Guide to Games, The (2008), by Bart King. An updated version of a 1909 book titled *Games for the Playground, Home, School and Gymnasium*. Includes active games (e.g., Bacon!, Bull in the Ring, Centipede Tag, Forcing the City Gates, Good vs. Evil, Hot Lava Monster, Decapitation Frisbee), quiet games (iPod People, Kaleidoscope, Scat), and beanbag and ball games (Chuck and Run, Double-Death Corner Ball, Paranoia Ball).

Zoom Catalog, The (1972), by WGBH Educational Foundation. Jokes, poems, crafts, and other fun ideas contributed by young fans of the 1972–78 PBS kids' show *Zoom*. Includes such low-tech games as Statues, Ha-Ha, Hockey Card, Zzzz, Poor Kitty, and Pass and Sing. A charming, loosely designed collection that helped inspire the original *Unbored* book.

Home Games

@AboutBoardGames. If you're a boardgame addict, fiending for news about games that haven't reached your local game store yet, or updates to your favorite games, check out this Twitter feed from About.com's boardgame and card game expert, Erik Arneson.

Be the Coolest Dad on the Block (2005), by Simon Rose and Steve Caplin. Features games like Tennis Cricket, the Flippin' Fish, Ibble Dibble, and the Jell-O Game. Plus a Viking game called Kubb... which was once played with the bones of defeated warriors! Not just for dads.

BenandBirdy.blogspot.com. Catherine Newman, who is one of this book's contributors, blogs about her family's obsessions—one of which is boardgames. Her reviews of strategy games, games that are about speed and dexterity, games for younger children, party games, and travel games are extremely helpful.

BoardGameGeek.com. Here you'll find information about tens of thousands of games, and you can see which ones are the most popular among the site's users—

who also vote on annual Golden Geek Awards for games in such categories as Best Family Game, Best Children's Game, and Most Innovative Game. It takes a while to figure out the site's navigation, but it's worth it once you're doing specific searches based on game category (e.g., Bluffing, Math, Mythology, Puzzles, Trivia) and even game mechanic (Cooperative Play, Dice Rolling, Pattern Recognition). Not just for geeks.

Book of Parties and Pastimes, The (1912), by Mary Dawson and Emma Paddock Telford. Party and parlor games from a century ago, including Clothespin Fishing, Historical Art Game, Palindromes, and Literary Geography. They're extremely low-tech, and they're fun.

CardboardEdison.tumblr.com. A website linking to the brightest new ideas, from around the Web, that are of interest to boardgame inventors—and to those of us interested in what it takes to invent a boardgame. Everything you didn't know that you might need to know about boardgame playtesting and prototyping. The website's Twitter feed is @CardboardEdison.

DadsGamingAddiction.com. Boardgame and videogame reviews from Vincent Paone, who tests new games with his family members and then shares that experience with the rest of us. He's an early adopter—you'll hear about games here long before they make it to market.

DavidParlett.co.uk. David Parlett is a celebrated British game designer (e.g., *Hare & Tortoise*, *Ninety-Nine*) and game historian (the *Oxford History of*

Card Games, the *Oxford History of Board Games*). His website features the rules to dozens of games of all sorts that Parlett has created, as well as his (often quite scholarly) game-related writing.

Family Games: The 100 Best (2010), by James Lowder. Top game designers, including Alan R. Moon (*Ticket to Ride*), Matthew Kirby (*Apples to Apples*), Richard Garfield (*Magic: The Gathering*), and Susan McKinley Ross (*Qwirkle*), write about their favorite board games, card games, miniatures games, and roleplaying games, including some that are very obscure.

Fun and Games for the 21st Century Family (2010), by Steve Caplin and Simon Rose. Over 100 games, some of which are "from the archives" (traditional British games that require no electrical power, e.g., Flipping Kipper, Eat the Jelly), but most of which call for a computer with internet access and/or a smartphone. The game Churchill's War, for example, uses Google's search function to test players' knowledge of the lives of the famous; Carnelli and Endless Words, meanwhile, are parlor games played via IM.

Geek Dad (2010), by Ken Denmead. DIY projects from the blog GeekDad.com, including a build-it-yourself boardgame called Buildrz; a demolition derby game involving remote control cars, LEGO bricks, and hot glue guns; outdoor videogame-like games; and a role-playing game in which kids earn attribute points from their parents for doing chores and other feats. The sequel is *Geek Dad's Guide to Weekend Fun* (2011). Not just for dads.

Geek Mom (2012), by Natania Barron, Kathy Ceceri, Corrina Lawson, Jenny Williams. Projects, tips, adventures, and games—including One Thousand Blank White Cards, the topological game Tic-Tac-Torus, and Secret Agent Man—for geek moms and their families. Also see their website: Geek-Mom.com/tag/board-games. Not just for moms.

Great Games! 175 Games & Activities for Families, Groups, & Children (2009), by Matthew Toone. Here you'll find the rules to family and group games such as Mafia, Psychiatrist, Who's the Smartest?, Frisbee Baseball, and Murderer in the Dark, plus variations and new games.

Great Games for Great Parties (1991), by Andrea Campbell. Every kind of party game from quiet games to relays and stunts, to hunts and musical games. Includes a useful chapter on techniques for leading party games at parties—e.g., making yourself visible, giving concise instructions, assessing the progress of the game, and deciding when the game is over.

Parlour Games for Modern Families (US edition, 2012), by Myfanwy Jones and Spiri Tsintziras. Dozens of free, unplugged, creative after-dinner activities—from writing and drawing games (Squiggle, Redondo, Tapatan) and games of motion and make-believe (Burglars, Mafia, Hagoo) to card and dice games (Snap, Pig, Farkle) and games spoken aloud (Crambo, Carnelli, Taboo). Of the many anthologies of parlor games out there, this one is our favorite.

Game Changers

1000 PlayThinks: Puzzles, Paradoxes, Illusions & Games (2001), by Ivan Moscovich. Brain-boosting games related to geometry, points and lines, graphs and networks, curves and circles, shapes and polygons, patterns, dissections, numbers, logic and probability, topology, and perception.

Best New Games (2002), by Dale N. Le Fevre. In the 1970s, the New Games Foundation invented and inspired dozens of cooperative group interactive games that are done just for fun, and that are for everybody regardless of age, size, gender, or ability level. These "New Games" sometimes include competition, but anybody can win. The author of this book has used New Games to promote understanding between Jews and Arabs in Israel, Protestants and Catholics in Northern Ireland, and Croats, Serbs, and Muslims in Croatia and Serbia.

Board Game Education, A (2009), by Jeffrey P. Hinebaugh. The author offers pointers on modifying boardgames that you probably already own into games that enhance important educational skills and concepts. Even games for young kids can be brain-boosters: *Candy Land*, for example, can be modified into a strategy game; and *Chutes and Ladders* can be used to learn algebraic equations and advanced math.

CoachesAcrossContinents. org. A nonprofit that promotes cultural understanding and international social justice through soccer.

Critical Play (2009), by Mary Flanagan. A scholarly book—by the founder of Tiltfactor, a game research laboratory at Dartmouth College—which explores the ways in which games can be a means for creative expression, instruments for conceptual thinking, and tools for social change. She encourages game designers to subvert gaming culture's usual norms.

Gameful.org. A social network for game developers interested in using games for social good... or, as they describe themselves, "a Secret HQ for Worldchanging Game Developers." The go-to place for discussions on creating games that make us happier, smarter, stronger, healthier, more collaborative, more creative, and better connected to our friends and family.

Gamelab.mit.edu. The MIT Game Lab brings together scholars, game designers, and technologists to explore what happens when endeavors— from entertainment to education, art to activism, science to socialization—are "gamified." The Game Lab develops games, does playtesting research, studies the culture of gaming, and more.

GamesForChange.org. Games for Change facilitates the creation and distribution of "social impact games"—that is, games which can serve as critical tools in humanitarian and educational efforts. Their annual Games for Change Festival is the leading event uniting "games for change" creators with groups who might want to use them. Twitter feed: @G4C.

GamesForHealth.org. A community that brings together game developers and health care professionals, in order to develop games that improve health (e.g., by increasing activity) and the delivery of health care (by improving hospital operations and training healthcare providers).

GamesLearningSociety.org. The organization Games Learning Society believes that the power of videogames can be harnessed to transform learning—and maybe society, too. The website features innovative videogames, which were developed by the GLS, that promote learning about various STEM (science, technology, engineering, and mathematics) topics.

GetWellGamers.org. The Get-Well Gamers Foundation brings videogame systems and games to children's hospitals—because videogames are an effective pain management tool.

Junkyard Sports (2005), by Bernie DeKoven. The author, a theorist of fun who in the 1970s directed the New Games Foundation, offers the rules to 75 "junkyard sports" games, most of which mash up two sports games whose rules you already know. For example: Beach-Basket Soccer, Chess Football, Racket Basket, Dodgeball Baseball, and Frisbee Hockey.

New Games Book, The (1976), by the New Games Foundation. A cult classic that helped introduce the play-hard, play-fair, nobody-hurt "New Games" trend to the world. Includes games for two (Tweezli-Whop, Schmerltz, Fraha), games for a dozen (Human Pinball, Smaug's

Jewels, LummiSticks), and games for large groups (Earthball, AmoebaRace, Blob).

Reality is Broken: Why Games Make Us Better and How They Can Change the World (2011), by Jane McGonigal. The author, a prominent alternate reality game designer, argues that videogames are so popular because they fulfill genuine human needs... and that we can use the lessons of game design to fix what is wrong with the real world.

Silver Bullets: A Guide to Initiative Problems, Adventure Games, Stunts and Trust Activities (1984), by Karl Rohnke. Dozens of games (Balloon Frantic, Ultimate Comet Ball, Samurai), trust exercises (Trust Dive, Sherpa Walk), initiatives (Nitro Crossing, Rabid Nugget Rescue), and stunts (People-to-People Surfing, Compass Walk) aimed at increasing the players' sense of personal confidence, players' agility, and—importantly—mutual support within a group.

SeriousGames.org. The Serious Games Initiative aims to connect developers from the electronic game industry with "serious games" projects involving the use of games in education, training, health, and public policy.

World Peace and Other 4th-Grade Achievements (2013), by John Hunter. A look inside the creation of the World Peace Game, which Hunter created to help elementary, middle, and high school students think about solving some of our most difficult real-world challenges.

Adventure Games

175 Best Camp Games, The (2009), by Kathleen, Laura & Mary Fraser. Games for breaking the ice (Life Raft, Human Knot), games for taking it easy (Total Recall, Dumb Crambo), improv games (Freeze, Bus Stop), overnight games (Werewolf Tag, One-Word Story), get-moving games (Parachute Golf, SPUD), musical games (Rikki Tikki, Star Strike), wet and wild games (Firefighter Relay, Torpedo), plus plenty of old-fashioned camp games.

1001 Video Games You Must Play Before You Die (2010), by Tony Mott. The first, most comprehensive, and only critical guide to videogames ever published. Offers a history of videogames from the 1970s through the early 2000s—including arcade games, home console games, portable games and computer games. Includes vintage screen shots, which are fun to see.

Adventurous Book of Outdoor Games, The (2008), by Scott Strother. As today's grownups start to forget the rules of the games they grew up playing—from Bombardment to Cops and Robbers, to Kick the Can and Wall Ball—this book offers a little assistance.

Apps for Kids (boingboing. net/tag/appsforkids). A short, entertaining weekly podcast in which Mark Frauenfelder, editor of the magazine *MAKE*, and his daughter Jane discuss their favorite smartphone and tablet apps. You can subscribe to the podcast via the iTunes store.

Apps Gone Free. An app that directs you to smartphone games that are temporarily being given away for free (for promotional purposes). 'Nuff said. Twitter feed: @AppsGoneFree.

Botlogic.us. This online puzzle game (at botlogic.us) challenges kids to apply programming concepts to complex logic problems. Using simple code, program your bot to navigate through mazes that get progressively harder. As your skills improve, you can earn rewards by using the fewest number of commands—and compete with friends in tournaments.

ComeOutAndPlay.org. Come Out & Play is an annual festival of street games that turns New York City & San Francisco into a giant playground. The festival provides a forum for new types of public games and play by bringing together players eager to interact with the world around them and designers producing innovative new games and experiences.

CraftyRichela.com. The website of *Tape It & Make It* and *Tape It & Make It More* author Richela Fabian Morgan, who is a contributor to this book. Download patterns that are used in her most popular projects.

Google Earth Hacks. This website (gearthhacks.com) is created by users of Google Earth (which lets you view the entire earth in 3D—and in close detail), who've figured out ways to enhance your Google Earth experience, including games.

How to Do Nothing with Nobody All Alone by Yourself (1958, reissued in 2010), by Robert Paul Smith. This book includes a section with detailed instructions on how to play the 1920s-era game Mumbly-Peg, which involves flipping a knife with an awl (a thin blade for punching holes in leather) out of your hand into the ground. Includes Mumbly-Peg variants.

Leaving Mundania: Inside the Transformative World of Live Action Role-Playing Games (2012), by Lizzie Stark. Live action role playing (aka larping) can be as simple as running around in the woods with some friends, pretending to be elves and dwarves on a quest. If you're interested in involved larping, here's everything you could want to know about boffers, farbs, ganking, min-maxers, munchkins, and norms.

Multicultural Game Book, The: More than 70 Traditional Games from 30 Countries (1993, 1999), by Louise Orlando. Kids' games from Africa (e.g., Botswana, Egypt, and Zaire), Asia (Afghanistan, Russia, China, India, Japan, Vietnam), Australia and New Zealand, Europe (Denmark, France, Ireland, Spain), North America (Canada, Mexico, United States), and South America (Brazil, Chile).

Play with Us: 100 Games from Around the World (2005), by Oriol Ripoll. Although the book's illustrations are geared towards younger kids, its activities—including games of tag, games of strength, games of chance, hand games, ball games, and more—are fun for all ages. The games hail from Afghanistan, Brazil, Colombia, El Salvador, France, Ghana, India, Israel, Japan, Laos, Mexico, Mongolia, Morocco, Scotland, and Tibet.

RPGs for Kids. A website (tlucretius.net/RPGs/kids.html) offering reviews of role playing games intended for kids (e.g., *Mouse Guard RPG*), as well as RPGs for all ages (*Usagi Yojimbo RPG*), as well as RPGs that can be tweaked for kids—like *Pokethulu*, which combines aspects of the Pokémon story with aspects of H.P. Lovecraft's Cthulhu mythos.

Scratch. Not only a programming language that allows kids to create and share their own videogames by dragging and dropping LEGO-style bricks of code, but a community website (scratch.mit.edu) in which you can swap ideas. A free project from MIT's Media Lab.

Super Scratch Programming Adventure!: Learn to Program By Making Cool Games (2012), by The LEAD Project. Learn programming fundamentals as you make your own videogames using Scratch. The book offers step-by-step explanations of the code, plus fun challenges.

Tynker. Inspired by Scratch, Tynker makes it fun and easy for kids to learn programming—by making games. They offer interactive courses to learn programming at school and at home. Their website: tynker.com. Their Twitter feed: @gotynker.

INDEX

TEAM UNBORED

Joshua Glenn is cofounder of the website HiLobrow, and coauthor and coeditor of several books. He has worked as a newspaper, magazine, and website editor; and he was a columnist for *The Boston Globe*. During the 1990s he published the zine/journal *Hermenaut*. He lives in Boston with his wife and sons.

Heather Kasunick teaches visual arts in a public high school. She has exhibited at the Brattleboro Museum and Art Center, the Fitchburg Museum of Art, and The MPG Contemporary Gallery (Boston), among other venues. She lives in Northampton, Mass., with her husband and their dog. More info: wondercupboard.blogspot.com.

Elizabeth Foy Larsen is a writer and editor whose stories on children and families have appeared in *The New York Times*, *Mother Jones*, and *Parents*. She has worked as a newspaper, magazine, and website editor. In the 1990s, she was a member of the team that launched *Sassy*, a magazine for teen girls. She lives in Minneapolis with her husband, daughter, and two sons.

Tony Leone is principal of Leone Design, a graphic design studio and consultancy in Boston. His work has been honored by the American Institute of Graphic Arts, and has been featured in *Communication Arts*, *Print*, *Graphis*, and elsewhere. During the 1990s he was the art director of the zine/journal *Hermenaut*. He lives in Boston with his wife, son, and daughter.

Chris Piascik is a freelance designer and illustrator from Connecticut who recently held his sixth solo exhibition. For the past four years, he has been posting daily drawings to his website; in 2012, he self-published a book of the first thousand drawings. More info: chrispiascik.com.

Mister Reusch has made illustrations for Burton Snowboards, Harmonix Rock Band, StrideRite, and others; he has work featured in books about rock poster art and tattoo designs. He teaches illustration at Massachusetts College of Art & Design in Boston. He lives in Haverhill, Mass., with his girlfriend and their dogs. More info: misterreusch.com.

GO, DESIGN TEAM! Our book *Unbored: The Essential Field Guide to Serious Fun* won three prestigious design awards: *Print* magazine's Regional Design Annual, *HOW* magazine's International Design Annual, and the AIGA's Best of New England (BoNE) Show.

CONTRIBUTORS

Joe Alterio is an art director, illustrator, animator, comic creator, and artist. He has made art and comics for the *New York Times*, *The Atlantic*, and *Rolling Stone*; and he is the founder of Robots + Monsters, an organization that raised money for charity by selling custom-made drawings. He lives in Seattle with his wife and son. More info: JoeAlterio.com.

Patrick Cates is a computer boffin, writer and puzzle addict who hails from London, where the crosswords are cryptic and the riddles are recondite. He lives in Los Angeles with his wife and daughter, who both serve as guinea pigs for his word game experiments. Follow @modussolvendi on Twitter.

Chris Dahlen was the writer on Klei Entertainment's stealth videogame *Mark of the Ninja*. He has covered music, games, and tech for *Pitchfork*, *Variety*, *Polygon*, and *Kill Screen*, where he served as co-founder and editor-in-chief. He lives in Portsmouth, N.H., with his wife and son. More info: SavetheRobot.com.

Stephen Duncombe is author and editor of six books, including *Dream: Re-Imagining Progressive Politics in an Age of Fantasy* and a digital edition of Thomas More's *Utopia*. He is the co-founder of the Center for Artistic Activism. He lives in New York City with his wife, Jean Railla, and their two game-loving boys. More info: ArtisticActivism.org.

Richela Fabian Morgan is an indie crafter, craft instructor, and author of the #1 bestseller duct tape craft book *Tape It & Make It*, its sequel, *Tape It & Make More*, and *The Green Crafter*. She lives in Larchmont, New York, with her husband and two crafty kids. More info: RichelaFabianMorgan.com.

Catherine Newman is the author of the book *Waiting for Birdy* and the blog Ben & Birdy. She writes for *FamilyFun* and other magazines, edits the nonprofit kids' cooking magazine *ChopChop*, and is the etiquette columnist at *Real Simple*. She lives with her family in Amherst, Mass. More info: BenandBirdy.blogspot.com.

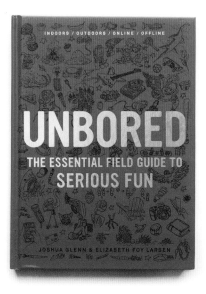